Alzheimer's

*Finding
the Words*

HARRIET HODGSON

CHRONIMED
PUBLISHING

Library of Congress Cataloging-in-Publication Data

Hodgson, Harriet W.
Alzheimers: Finding the Words/by Harriet Hodson.
    p.   c.m.

Includes bibliographical references and index.
ISBN 1-56561-071-7

    1. Alzheimer's disease—Patients—Language.
    2.   Interpersonal communication. 3. Alzheimer's
disease—Patients—Care. 4. Alzheimer's disease—
Patients—Family relationships.
    I. Title.

RC523.H63   1995
616.8'31—dc20   95—12869
                  CIP

Edited by Donna Hoel
Cover design: Garborg Design Works
Text Design: Janet Hogge
Printed in the United States of America

Published by
CHRONIMED Publishing
P.O. Box 59032
Minneapolis, MN 55459-9686

This book is dedicated to my mother,
Mabel Clifton Weil,
a funny, elegant,
and wise woman.

———————

Just think of the changes I've seen.
When I was a child I went to school
in a horse-drawn carriage.
When I was an adult I saw men
walk on the moon.
I think I've lived my life
at the best time.

—Mabel Clifton Weil

———————————

CONTENTS

PREFACE

In 1982, the morning after my father died, my mother had a mini-stroke in her sleep. Doctors call these strokes TIA.s, which is short for transient ischemic attacks. Her older sister, who had come to be with Mom, attributed her confusion to "sleeping hard."

With the clarity of hindsight, I now realize this stroke was the beginning of Mom's decline. Confused, stressed, and grieving, Mom sold the house on Long Island and moved to Melbourne, Florida, to be near her sister. I became a long-distance caregiver. Caring for someone who lives thousands of miles away is almost impossible.

Family problems prevented me from visiting Mom for a time. However, I called her regularly and she called me. Hearing Mom's voice always made me happy, but I became increasingly unhappy about the events she described. Mom seemed to have lost her common sense.

For example, Mom was asked to bake banana bread for the coffee hour following the morning church service. Pleased by the request, she baked the bread and left for church early. Only she didn't know her mental clock was off by 12 hours.

"I waited in the parking lot and nobody came," she admitted. "When the moon came out I knew it was night."

After a series of failed attempts, Mom finally passed her driver's test. She bought a new compact car.

When Mom took the car in for its three-month check, an unscrupulous salesperson sold her another new car off the showroom floor, a "loaded" Cougar with leather seats, a computerized dashboard, and oversized racing tires.

"It's the kind of car kids drive," Mom said proudly.

The word "travel" became Mom's middle name. She went on an Alaskan cruise, visited western parks, took Elderhostel courses, and flew to foreign lands. One Saturday morning, Mom called to tell me she had returned from "the city with all the boats."

"What city?" I asked.

"I don't know," Mom said.

"San Diego?" I asked hopefully.

"N-o-o-o-o," Mom said, drawing out the word. "It was across the ocean."

"Venice?"

"Yes, that's where I was," she answered cheerfully. "I bought glass vases."

During our phone conversations, Mom often bragged about her driving. "I really know how to step on it!" she exclaimed. All too clearly, I could picture an 85-year-old, white haired grandmother with a "lead foot" racing around town. Mom got so many speeding tickets the judge knew her by name.

One day, blinded by sunlight, Mom pulled out into an intersection directly in front of another car. The crash put Mom in the hospital for a week. I called Mom and pleaded with her to move to Minnesota. She refused.

Trying another tack, I asked Mom if she would promise to give up driving and use cabs.

"No, I won't," she said firmly.

As usual, we invited Mom to Minnesota for the holidays. On Christmas morning Mom gave my husband a light bulb and I received chipped rummage sale goods. I called my brother in New York to voice my concerns. "Hey, I got a little girl's sweater," he said, struggling to control his sadness.

The gifts upset me so much I contacted a cousin who lived near Mom. He and his wife kindly volunteered to keep an eye on Mom and continue taking her out for dinner. Downstairs neighbors "adopted" her and checked on her often. My brother and I visited Florida to see how she was doing.

Things were quiet until one day Mom was found wandering in a department store. A clerk asked if she needed help. "I told her I was looking for my car," Mom recalled. "She said cars aren't parked inside the store; they're parked outside in the lot. They called the manager of my complex, and he came and got me."

I gave Mom a few seconds to gather her thoughts. "It's time to move to Minnesota," I said.

"Well, that *was* a scary experience," Mom admitted. "I guess I'll come."

We developed a plan: my husband and I would go to Melbourne, pack Mom's goods, contact a mover, arrange for a tag sale, return on moving weekend, and drive the Cougar back to our home. Just thinking about the plan made me tired.

Any doubts I had about moving Mom vanished the minute I walked in the door. The apartment smelled like garbage, and every surface was piled with junk. Odd shoes, newspapers, and trash covered the floor. Greeting cards and reminder notes were taped to the walls like giant confetti. Furniture was draped with blouses, sweaters, underwear, skirts, slacks, and panty-hose. I felt like I had stepped into a surrealist painting.

Early the next morning, my husband and I started packing. I packed dishes while he sorted through Mom's legal papers. A few hours later my husband walked into the kitchen, a file folder in his hands, his face ashen. "Your Mom's cash is gone," he said. "There's nothing in her bank account."

It seems Mom had fallen for every scam: "gift" life insurance, hospital bed, magazines, perfume club, lotteries, bulk vitamins, limited editions, product "testing," overpriced water filtration, etc. Worse, Mom had forgotten to pay her taxes. Did she have Alzheimer's disease? The question loomed in my mind all weekend and on the way home.

After a lot of thought, I decided the answer didn't make any difference. Several years ago Mom had a computerized tomogram (CT scan) at the Mayo Clinic. The resulting photo, which looked like Swiss cheese, clearly showed the stroke damage to her brain.

Mom moved into an assisted-living community two and a half miles from our house. Now I could observe her closely. Sometimes angry, sometimes sullen, Mom's behavior was erratic to say the least. The two dominant traits of her personality—intelligence and humor—had all but vanished.

Mom has lived here now for more than five years. Since the move, she has had another mini-stroke (she drags her right foot slightly) and shoulder surgery (she has a metal shoulder socket). She's developed diabetes and every symptom of Alzheimer's disease. As her daughter, caregiver, and power of attorney, I have observed Mom's failing health firsthand.

Witnessing her failing speech has been as painful as seeing her failing health. I have decoded word substitutions, waited for time delays, noted transmission and reception errors, deflected emotional outbursts, and endured long periods of silence. I kept asking myself what could I do to improve communication?

Many books have been written about Alzheimer's disease, but none of them was what I wanted. I wanted the latest information on communicating with Alzheimer's patients—not sterile research. I wanted practical tips based on life experience. As I adapted my speech to Mom's mental ability, this book took shape in my mind.

Research is the first step in writing any nonfiction book. I clipped magazine articles, read journal articles on Alzheimer's, searched computer databases, talked with other caregivers, and attended a Mayo Clinic conference. Outlining the book was the next step. So far so good. When the time came to start the actual writing, however, I had serious misgivings.

How would Mom respond to the book? I didn't want to hurt my mother or denigrate the woman she had been. And deep in my heart I thought Mom would die while the book was in progress. My worries kept me awake at night and kept me from writing as well.

The day before I planned to start the book, I had Mom over for lunch. Between bites of her sandwich, she commented on the pink flowers and green grass outside the kitchen window. "I wonder what happened to Esther?" she asked suddenly.

Thinking of my former neighbor brought a smile to my face. Dear, sweet, kind Esther, a nurse, had died about 20 years ago. Perhaps Mom wanted to talk about the hereafter. I decided to proceed cautiously. "Why do you ask?" I replied.

"Well, Esther is such an active person. I wonder what she's doing," said Mom.

"Esther died many years ago," I said quietly.

"I don't remember that," Mom said, shaking her head. For a few moments she was lost in thought. "I think your father had a sister named Clara, and she died, too."

"You're right, Mom," I said.

Painful as it was, our lunchtime talk convinced me Mom was in the severe stage of Alzheimer's disease. She is incapable of understanding a detailed magazine article, let alone a book. There are millions of Alzheimer's patients like Mom and millions of caregivers like me.

All caregivers, whether we are family members or health professionals, rely on speech. We face a daily dilemma: How do you communicate with a failing mind? How do you care for yourself in the process?

I wrote this book to help caregivers communicate with Alzheimer's patients. Each chapter focuses on a different aspect of communication. For easy reference, I have included headings and subheadings. Examples from my mother's life bring these issues to life.

While my mother is just one patient, she is, in a symbolic sense, every Alzheimer's patient. A doctor would describe Mom's disease as a classic "textbook case." Although Alzheimer's patients can no longer learn, we can still learn from them.

Perhaps the greatest lesson we learn, or relearn, is respect for human dignity. Improving communication is a way of showing our respect. Alzheimer's is a fatal disease. Until the end comes, we can savor life, do our best, and speak with tender voices.

CHAPTER 1

How Alzheimer's Affects Speech

Topics

Defining Alzheimer's Disease

Early Warning Signs

Ten Crucial Symptoms

Getting An Evaluation

Probable Alzheimer's Disease

Stages of the Disease

Changes in the Early Stage

Changes in the Moderate Stage

Changes in the Severe Stage

Changes in the Final Stage

Why Caregivers Have Trouble

Observe, Observe!

Defining Alzheimer's Disease

An overview brochure published by the Alzheimer's Association defines the disease as progressive and degenerative—a disease "in which brain cells die and are not replaced." The results are impaired memory, thinking, and behavior.

To me, the most curious thing about Alzheimer's disease is the people who have it don't know it. Mom believes her brain is functioning with clock-like precision. It isn't. According to *Alzheimer's: A Caregiver's Guide and Sourcebook* the disease damages the cortex of the brain.

Patients lose the ability to understand definitions, compare similarities and differences, make word associations, or use descriptive language. An extensive vocabulary may be reduced to a few dozen words. In short, caregivers and patients no longer speak the same language.

Early Warning Signs

Word Substitutions

Alzheimer's disease has many early warning signs and word substitutions are one of the first. The patient may say jar for vase, book for magazine, or coat for robe. These substitutions are easy to understand because the words are related. As Alzheimer's disease progresses, however, the number of substitutions increases.

One word substitution in a sentence is easy to decode. Three or four substitutions in a sentence are another matter entirely. If you can't figure out the meaning of a sentence, your response will probably be off course. Conversations with Alzheimer's patients may be reduced to "baffle-gab."

Loss of Expressive Language

The next early warning sign is the inability to describe feelings and experiences. Despite an acute desire to express himself or herself, the patient can't do it and may stop talking in the middle of a sentence. Both patients and caregivers are frustrated by this loss of language.

I realized Mom's sentences were becoming shorter, often mere nouns and verbs, without any adjectives at all. These short sentences made her conversation abrupt, and harsh comments became even harsher. The poet Ogden Nash might have described Mom's speech as "terse verse."

Mom just couldn't come up with the words she wanted. Let me give you an example. One evening Mom went to the ballet with other retirement community residents. The performance touched Mom deeply but she couldn't convey her feelings to me.

"It was so beautiful. . . . " Mom paused and tried again. "It was so beautiful that . . . ." She sighed in frustration, and tears glistened in her eyes. "Well, I didn't know whether to clap or cry," Mom said and quickly changed the subject.

Unless we're careful, the loss of expressive language can distance patients and caregivers. The patient doesn't realize the problem and may think he or she has done something wrong. We can encourage description by giving leads such as, "What color were the costumes?"

Messiness

Messiness is also an early warning sign of Alzheimer's disease. The parent who used to have high standards of cleanliness may turn into a slob, wearing messy clothes and living in a messy place. Alzheimer's patients tend to use similar excuses to explain their messiness.

Excuse 1—*"I'm too busy."*

Aunt Sadie may lead a passive, quiet life, but she doesn't think she has the time to tidy up. If the truth were known, Aunt Sadie is having trouble keeping track of life's basics—food, clothing, and shelter.

Excuse 2— *"I live alone."*

The basis of this excuse is that nobody else sees the mess, therefore it doesn't matter. This excuse totally discounts personal hygiene and safety. Messiness contributes to one of the most common injuries among the elderly, hip fractures, which are often fatal.

Excuse 3—*"Why bother?"*

When I asked my mother why she didn't make her bed, she replied, "Why? I'm only going to get in it again." Caregivers need to be alert to this kind of thinking, which can be a sign of depression. The next chapter contains more information on this topic.

Forgetfulness

Another early sign of Alzheimer's disease is forgetfulness. The patient may not know the date, run out of groceries, or begin to wander. One grandmother drove to town and forgot why she was there. Thank goodness this person had enough sense to drive home again.

Stress, grief, and illness can make anyone forgetful. But if your loved one forgets things daily, an alarm as loud as any fire siren should go off in your head. Chances are this isn't the absent-mindedness that comes with aging; it's mental impairment caused by disease. Forgetfulness leads straight to the next early warning sign, cover-ups.

Cover-Ups

With all of these difficulties, it's hard to believe that Alzheimer's patients have the ability to cover-up. But they do. Often they will blame the caregiver for the forgetfulness. For example, one day Mom forgot we were going out to lunch. I waited 20 minutes for her, but she didn't appear.

Because the elevators were crowded, I asked the receptionist to call her. She said Mom sounded sleepy but would be down shortly. A few minutes later, Mom emerged from the elevator wearing a rumpled outfit, the wrinkled imprint of a pillowcase on her cheek.

"You didn't tell me we were meeting in the lobby," she said angrily. "I would have come down."

Cover-ups may be verbal, as with the above example, or they may use physical props. The patient may carry a book around to "prove" he or she can read. But eventually patients who have Alzheimer's disease lose the ability to cover-up anything.

Ten Crucial Symptoms

Alzheimer's disease has 10 crucial symptoms. A list of these symptoms appears in an Alzheimer's Association brochure entitled *"Is It Alzheimer's?"* I have altered the list slightly and added explanatory comments.

1. Recent memory loss (computer skills, running a household, etc.)

2. Difficulty with familiar tasks (such as dressing, cooking, and driving)

3. Speech problems (telling the same stories over and over again, drifting off during conversation)

4. Time and place mix-ups (like Mom going to the morning church service at night)

5. Poor judgment (leaving doors unlocked, standing nude in front of windows, not wearing a coat in winter, etc.)

6. Trouble with abstract thinking (difficulty with cause and effect reasoning, inability to understand analogies)

7. Misplacing or losing things (including the tendency to squirrel things away in odd places)

8. Changes in mood and behavior (treating loved ones like strangers)

9. Personality changes (emotional outbursts, quickly shifting from gentle to hostile, etc.)

10. Loss of motivation (generally passive behavior and the constant desire to sleep)

If I have any advice for caregivers, it's trust your instincts—those inner messages that tell you something is wrong. Family members often pick up on Alzheimer's disease before health professionals do. Moreover, some health professionals may try to talk you out of your diagnosis.

Usually, Alzheimer's disease strikes people in their 70s, 80s, and 90s. However, the Alzheimer's Association reports a documented case in a 28-year-old person. Whether you're 28 or 88, this is one of the cruelest diseases known to humankind.

Alzheimer's disease can turn a loving parent into an adversary, a mature grandmother into a child, a friendly neighbor into a bully. The rate of mental deterioration varies from person to person. Some Alzheimer's patients remain at the same level for years, whereas others deteriorate within months.

Getting An Evaluation:

Physical Exam

An Alzheimer's evaluation begins with a complete physical exam. In addition to assessing the patient's overall health, the doctor will look for other diseases that could affect thinking, such as a brain tumor, arterial disease, or diabetes. A neurological work-up is part of the physical exam.

The doctor will probably order a chest x-ray, computerized tomogram (CT scan), and magnetic resonance imaging (MRI) to rule out other treatable diseases. Additional tests, such as drug levels, toxic screening, psychometrics (intelligence or psychological tests), may also be ordered.

Mental Assessments

Doctors can learn a lot about a patient's mental state from simple tests. One of these is the "draw-a-clock" test. First, the patient is asked to draw a clock face. Patients who have Alzheimer's may not be able to draw a circle at all. The circle may be an ellipse, a coil, or lines.

Next, the patient is asked to represent a specific time on the clock, say seven o'clock. This may generate a variety of responses. Samples of clock drawings are pictured in the article, "Clock Drawing in Alzheimer's Disease" by Trey Sunderland, M.D., and his colleagues.

In the article, samples are arranged from "best" to "worst." One clock face doesn't have any numbers on it. Instead, the numbers hang down from the right side of the clock like a lumpy balloon string. Another clock face has hands but no numbers. The "worst" clock looks like scribbles.

The house-drawing test is similar to the clock-drawing test. It starts with the patient being asked to draw a basic house shape. The doctor then asks the patient to draw doors and windows on the house. This test also generates a variety of responses in patients with Alzheimer's.

For example, the walls of the house may not meet. Doors and windows may be floating in space, rather than part of the house. Simple as these tests are, the house-drawing and clock-drawing tests have proven to be very reliable. Unfortunately, some doctors don't know about them.

Another relatively simple test is the Mini-Mental State Exam, included in an article by Dr. Martin Samuels in *Emergency Medicine.* The test begins with simple orientation questions about the year, season, date, day, and month.

Naming objects selected by the examiner comes next. This section is followed by attention and calculation questions—counting by sevens and spelling "world" backwards. A recall section, which consists of naming the objects used earlier, comes next.

Language is the last category of the exam. Tasks in this category include pointing to and naming objects, repeating a phrase, and following a three-stage command. The patient is also asked to read, write with eyes open and eyes closed, and copy a geometric figure.

Memory Evaluation

A trained professional will administer one or more mental assessments. Elizabeth Koss, Ph.D., the primary author of *Memory Evaluation in Alzheimer's Disease,* believes questionnaires are helpful evaluation tools. Questions from the "short-memory questionnaire" may challenge patients and caregivers alike.

One question asks if the patient can shop for five grocery items without a written list. Another asks if the patient can give someone directions to his or her home over the phone. Still another question asks if the patient remembers where his or her glasses are.

Reading the questions was daunting, for there have been times in my life, times of extraordinary stress, when I wouldn't have been able to answer any of them. Stress can make anyone forgetful, and being asked to take physical and mental tests can make patients feel stressed.

Neurologic Deficits

A trained professional will administer one or more tests to determine if the patient has any neurologic deficits that cause thinking problems. Robert J. Ivnik, Ph.D., a Mayo Clinic consultant and neuropsychologist, is an expert in these kinds of tests.

"Alzheimer's disease presents with a certain pattern of cognitive difficulty," Dr. Ivnik explained in a phone interview. Although there are no specific tests for Alzheimer's disease, he said psychological testing helps to answer three questions:

1. Is this person mentally impaired? (As opposed to the forgetfulness associated with normal aging.)

2. What is the specific nature of the impairment? (Testing can reveal which parts of the brain have been damaged.)

3. How can family members plan for the future? (Testing can indicate the rate of decline, which helps family members decide when to look for an assisted-living facility, nursing home, etc.)

According to Dr. Ivnik, testing should be done as early as possible. Broad assessments, such as I.Q. and tests for math and reading ability, are made first. Follow-up tests are then made, based on specific impairments.

Initial tests may include the Wechsler Adult Intelligence Scale-Revised (WAIS-R.) Some experts think these tests are invalid beyond age 74. However, Dr. Ivnik and other Mayo Clinic researchers have developed a series of statistical tables that adjust results for age.

Intelligence tests such as the Wechsler test are more formal, whereas the Boston Naming Test is less formal. This test consists of 60 line drawings of objects. The objects range from common things, such as a bed, to less common, such as a trellis. Patients are asked to name as many objects as possible and are scored accordingly.

"I would caution everyone that all tests require interpretation by a neuropsychologist," Dr. Ivnik said. We must also keep in mind that psychological tests don't give neurologic diagnoses.

Probable Alzheimer's Disease

The results of these mental and medical tests are sent to the patient's doctor. Based on this evidence, the doctor will determine if the patient has *probable* Alzheimer's disease. The word probable is used because an accurate diagnosis can only be made by examining the brain after death. Even so, getting an Alzheimer's evaluation is still worthwhile. According to the Alzheimer's Association, these evaluations are 80 to 90 percent accurate.

To conserve funds, Mom's doctor didn't put her through this extensive testing process. However, he believes Mom has Alzheimer's disease because all of the evidence points to this diagnosis.

Mom's health was also being monitored by a review board in her assisted-living community. Eventually, the review board determined it was time for her to transfer to the nursing care section of the community. I gave Mom the news in person. Nothing would be gained by telling her she had Alzheimer's, so I attributed her transfer to health problems.

Paramount in my mind was the fact that Mom had become a danger to herself. She kept leaving the stove burners on, setting off smoke alarms, falling down, forgetting to take her medicine, getting lost, and wandering at night. Any one of these symptoms could have proved fatal.

"I don't want to go to nursing care," Mom said.

"I know Mom," I soothed. "I wish I could turn back the clock and make us both young again. We'd ride into New York on the Long Island Railroad and go to stores and try on silly hats, just like we used to. But I can't do that. You have too many health problems."

Not surprisingly, Mom forgot about her health problems. Three days later, when Rochester's weather made the national news with a temperature of 32 below zero and a windchill factor of 76 below, Mom decided to return to Florida. "You don't want me anymore so I'm running away," she yelled over the phone.

If Mom fell outdoors she would freeze to death in minutes. I called her doctor, and he wrote special admittance orders for her. Dressed in Arctic gear—long underwear, down coats and mittens, and sturdy boots—my husband and I headed for Mom's apartment to escort her to nursing care.

The car engine balked, finally starting on the third try. At 10:30 at night, no other cars were on the road. Snow swirled across the highway and around street lights. It was so bitterly cold the air actually looked different, and the lights had iridescent circles around them, like the "sun dogs" Minnesotans see on subzero days.

Mom was wearing her bathrobe when she opened her apartment door. "What are you doing here?" she asked.

"You aren't taking good care of yourself," I blurted, "so we've come to escort you to nursing care."

Shocked as she was to see us, Mom drew herself up to her full height, retied the sash of her robe, and walked to the nursing care section of the building with quiet dignity.

When it was time for us to leave, we had to punch a numeric code into the exit door lock. As we left, I recalled a statement my mother had made earlier: "You can get into nursing care but you can't get out." I cried all the way home, and the tears froze on my face.

Stages of the Disease

Experts have divided Alzheimer's disease into four general stages: early, moderate, severe, and final. There isn't a clear line between the stages. Symptoms from one stage often "spill over" into another, which can be confusing for caretakers.

But one thing is clear. During every stage of Alzheimer's disease there is a decline in speech. In *Getting Through*, Elizabeth Ostuni and Mary Jo Santo Pietro divide the breakdown of speech into four categories: memory, comprehension, linguistic skills, and social communication.

According to Ostuni and Santo Pietro, "language differences are apparent almost from the onset of the disease." Because of this, you might want to keep a language diary to track the changes you observe. That's what I did. My observations helped me to adapt my speech to Mom's needs.

Changes in the Early Stage

Patients in the early stage of Alzheimer's forget recent conversations, appointments, ordinary words, and special dates, according to David Carroll, author of *When Your Loved One has Alzheimer's Disease*. I can't tell you how I felt when Mom blurted, "Somebody has a birthday this week. Who is it?"

"My birthday is on Friday," I said quietly.

"Oh," Mom said, gazing out the car window and humming to herself.

I wished I felt so carefree. Gripping the steering wheel tightly, it was all I could do not to burst into tears, but I knew that would confuse Mom and depress me. There would be plenty of time for tears later.

Some caregivers miss the early symptoms of declining speech, especially if the patient has detailed memories of the past. Don't be misled by these memories. Aunt Sadie, who is "sharp as a tack" and "never forgets a thing," may forget her address.

Carroll points out, however, that patients with Alzheimer's dementia can still carry on normal conversations. At least, the conversations seem normal to busy caregivers. Then too, you may not pick up on these signs if you don't see the patient regularly.

Changes in the Moderate Stage

Patients in the moderate stage of Alzheimer's disease lose the ability to count, spell, and remember plots. They also mismatch units of measurements with nouns, such as a dozen butter instead of a pound.

Decimal points or parts of numbers may be ignored. Instead of saying $20 the Alzheimer's patient may say $200. The patient may not include decimal points on checks. A $6.95 price tag may be interpreted as 95 cents. Errors like these obviously cause trouble at checkout counters and at the bank.

Around this time, the Alzheimer's patient may forget how to write his or her name. You may have difficulty making out a signature on a birthday card or reading a grocery list. Mom's bold signature has become wispy scratches on paper, the kind of writing that's called "a spidery hand" in novels.

According to Carroll, patients in the moderate stage of Alzheimer's can be noncommunicative. You can't see into the patient's head, so you have no idea of what he or she is thinking. Even an educated guess may be well off the mark.

All I can say is keep your sense of humor handy. If we didn't laugh, surely we would cry. A sense of humor helps caregivers keep life in balance. One smile can get us through the day. As one caregiver joked, "Alzheimer's must be catching. After I've been with Dad for an hour, I can hardly think!"

Changes in the Severe Stage

In the severe stage of Alzheimer's disease, patients may become angry and accusing. It's common for nursing home residents to report stolen food, clothing, and possessions. Though in some instances the claims are true, in most they are false.

Fights are easily ignited in this stage. An observer may think the fights are about nothing. I observed a fight like this. Two men, both in wheelchairs, approached each other in the hallway.

"You here again?" one challenged.

"Yeah and what's it to you?"

"Get out of here!"

"You get out of here!"

"Go to hell!"

"You go to hell!"

With that, each gave the other a glaring look and rolled his wheelchair in the opposite direction. This hostile exchange accomplished nothing other than venting feelings. Maybe that's what these two men needed to do.

Sometimes patients in the severe stage of Alzheimer's do not recognize their caregivers. Having a parent ask, "Who are you?" is one of the most painful experiences of life, a cruel joke played by nature. Aren't parents supposed to remember their children?

Changes in the Final Stage

Patients in the final stage of Alzheimer's have a near or total loss of speech. These people are so confused they can't remember from moment to moment. Carroll summarizes this stage in a short and painful sentence: "They are gone."

Any remaining speech may be repetitive. One nursing home resident keeps yelling, "Help me! Help me!" He doesn't remember that someone helped him only moments ago. Yelling "Help me!" may also be this patient's way of getting extra attention. Or these may be two of the few remaining words in his vocabulary.

Another nursing home resident searches for the number 13. Walking room to room, she peeks in the door and declares, "No 13 there." This woman also reads letters—not words—aloud from the newspaper.

"S-E-E," she says loudly. "Oh look, there are two E's."

Often patients in the final stage of Alzheimer's disease engage in repetitive humming or groaning. They may also rock in time to these sounds. Listening to this constant droning and watching repetitive motions can drive caregivers nuts.

At this stage, patients with Alzheimer's may revert to childlike behaviors. The patient may sing lullabies to a doll or want to be surrounded by stuffed animals at bedtime. This is the point of no return, the time when parents and children reverse roles forever. This is also the time when mourning begins in earnest.

Why Caregivers Have Trouble

In their book, *Getting Through*, Ostuni and Santo Pietro say patients in the final stage of Alzheimer's disease cannot create new memories. But I think that is precisely what caregivers are trying to do. I'm trying to sustain my mother's interest in life, ensure good medical care, and yes, create new memories.

Mom doesn't remember much, but she remembers her great-grandchildren. The twins, a boy and a girl, enrich her days. Every time she sees me she asks, "How are the twins?" My daughter keeps her supplied with photos and artwork. I suspect the twins are Mom's only reason for living.

So what's the bottom line? Caregivers have trouble talking to Alzheimer's patients and Alzheimer's patients have trouble talking to caregivers. Authors Donna Cohen, Ph.D., and Carl Eisdorfer, Ph.D., discuss communication difficulties in their book, *The Loss of Self*.

Part of the difficulty, they say, comes from the fact that the patient is less aware and less verbal. You can only guess what he or she is thinking. To make matters worse, patients may confuse the present with the past. Without accurate verbal clues, family and professional caregivers are lost.

The second part of the difficulty rests with the caregivers, according to Cohen and Eisdorfer. They write, "Many family members do not have a clear understanding of the patient's remaining strengths." How do we discover these strengths?

Observation is the key to answering this question. It's important to observe the patient over time. An adult son can't fly into town for the weekend and figure out what to do with dear old Dad. Working together, family and professional caregivers need to draw up a patient care plan and update the plan regularly.

Observe! Observe!

A patient's behavior can swing widely in a week. Perhaps this is where the expressions "having a good day" and "having a bad day" originated. It's important for family caregivers to keep professional caregivers informed. I kept track of the changes in Mom's health on a yellow legal pad. Some of the changes I noted:

- Bad rash on both legs.

- Didn't recognize Amy at Easter dinner (Amy is our younger daughter).

- Confuses day and night.

- Hides things—false teeth and medications.

- Unsafe—drops clothes and shoes anywhere.

- Forgets she has diabetes—binges on pies and cookies.

- Can't tell when something is wrong—slacks on backwards, not wearing a bra.

Using a phone became difficult for Mom. During one conversation she declared, "I can't think alone." Did she mean to say, "I can't think aloud?" Or had she made an unconscious admission? I don't know the answers to these questions and never will.

Much like a telephone, speech depends on transmission and reception. If there are problems on the line—Alzheimer's disease—the message is garbled. The sender and receiver are having entirely different conversations. That's why transmission errors are the focus of the next chapter.

CHAPTER 2

Changes in Speech Transmission

Topics

Functions of Speech

Types of Disorders

Speech Losses

Speech and Personality

Repetition

Tracking Subjects

Time Delays

Loss of Tact

Hurtful Speech

Aggressive Speech

Use of Refrains

Body Language/Gestures

Functions of Speech

The words we say reveal a lot about us. At a 1993 meeting in Rochester, Minnesota, Mayo Clinic Consultant Arnold Aaronson, Ph.D., discussed the functions of speech. A professor of speech pathology, Dr. Aaronson said speech was, first of all, an expression of ideas.

Unconscious ideas also influence speech and can be an indication of "something gone wrong" with our inner selves, Dr. Aaronson noted. Although his reference was to mental health, it may be applied to physical health as well. Changes in speech transmission give caregivers many clues as to what has "gone wrong" with Alzheimer's patients.

Often a patient's failing speech has a ripple effect on others. In *The 36-Hour Day,* authors Nancy Mace and Peter Rabins say caregivers may start to grieve for the patient because "we sense that language is the most human of mental skills." These diminishing mental skills are mirrored in diminishing speech.

Alzheimer's disease causes a variety of speech disorders, from repetition to mutism. Talking with patients becomes more difficult as the disorders progress. The patients may as well be talking a foreign language, so poor is our understanding.

Types of Disorders

The speech disorders caused by Alzheimer's disease may be grouped into five categories. These aren't the categories a neurologist would use, they're the categories a caregiver would use. Although each disorder has a medical name, I don't think the names are as important as the results.

The disorders add up to a series of "can't" experiences for patients. Here's a summary of speech disorders:

1. Recall—can't retrieve words or use them in a logical way.

2. Usage—can't link words together in sentences or group sentences together meaningfully; may include an inability to write.

3. Articulation—can't speak clearly; mixes up syllables and letters; may include voice loss.

4. Vision—can't read, interpret signs, or recognize letters of the alphabet.

5. Hearing—can't make sense of incoming speech or sounds, even with a hearing aid.

Since hearing and vision are essentially reception skills involving different neurological pathways, they are covered in the next chapter.

Many of us take speech for granted. Yet the ability to speak requires "a highly coordinated sequence of contractions of the respiratory musculature, larynx, pharynx, palate, tongue, and lips," observe Raymond Adams, M.D., and Maurice Victor, M.D., authors of *Principles of Neurology*.

Eventually patients lose the ability to make the necessary sequences to produce speech and movement. To put it simply, Alzheimer's disease short-circuits the brain's processing system. The brain may send out messages but, for complex neurological reasons, these messages aren't received by the appropriate part or parts of the body.

When body movement is involved, this loss of coordination is called apraxia. The Alzheimer's patient who has apraxia may forget how to use a fork and have to be fed. No matter how hard this person tries, he or she won't be able to use the fork. Losing this simple skill and others like it damages the patient's self-esteem.

Speech Losses

Aphasia

Aphasia is broadly defined as the inability to use words as symbols for speech. A doctor may summarize this condition by saying, "The patient can't talk." There are many types of aphasia.

In one type of aphasia, people often substitute syllables and letters in words. Dr. Bernard Alpers, author of *Clinical Neurology*, a medical school classic in the 1950s, called these kinds of substitutions "word hash." Certainly, word hash is difficult, if not impossible, for caregivers to decode. And word hash may become sentence hash. Even if you understand most of the words in a sentence, the sentence won't make sense. For example, "Did you (hum, hum, hum) anxious about O.K. I'll do it (pause) sing?"

Caregivers soon discover, however, that aphasic patients may still be able to swear "a blue streak." *Clinical Examinations in Neurology*, a textbook published by the Mayo Foundation for Education and Research, documents this point. It says, "The patient who is unable to voluntarily articulate a word beginning with the 'S' sound may be able to curse with clarity." Just what caregivers don't need!

Other patients may develop speech amnesia. This isn't the amnesia of television mysteries, in which the star tries to recall a past life; it's the inability to recall words. In *The Loss of Self*, Cohen and Eisdorfer note that these patients may be capable of making word associations.

"Individuals may lose the ability to say 'key' but make motions of turning a key in a lock," note the authors. After I read this quote I was reminded of a conversation I had with Mom. I had gone to visit her, and as she opened the door of her studio apartment, an acrid smell wafted into the hallway.

"What's burning?" I asked anxiously.

"Oh, I burned the toast," she explained. "That damn toaster always ruins my toast. But it's all right. I keep a bowl on the couch for the ceiling." What was she trying to tell me?

Over time, the apartment had become a real-life graph of Mom's mind—far worse than the Florida condominium, and I didn't think that was possible. It was so chaotic there was no place to sit (other than the bed) and that was barely visible. I scanned the apartment. There was a magazine on the couch directly beneath the smoke detector.

Translation: I keep a magazine handy to fan the smoke detector when it goes off. Every day, family and professional caregivers attempt to translate similar word substitutions. Sometimes we're right, sometimes we're wrong, and sometimes we're close, which adds to the confusion.

Slurred Speech

As Alzheimer's disease progresses, many patients develop slurred and slowed speech. The medical term for this is dysarthria, but some call the disorder "drunken speech" because the patient's tongue and lips aren't working properly.

Listening to these patients is like listening to a tape recording running at slow speed. The words may be so distorted you can barely understand them. Still, we can listen attentively, observe the patient's body language, and offer encouragement.

Speech therapy helps some of these patients, but it doesn't help all of them. The purpose of therapy is to strengthen the muscles used to produce speech. Patients in the final stage of Alzheimer's disease, however, can't remember speech exercises or perform them. The neurological damage is too great.

Loss of Voluntary Speech

Some Alzheimer's patients lose the ability to say words voluntarily, but the words they do say are still clear. Often the patient repeats the same word over and over. One patient chants the word "business" for hours on end, pausing only to take a breath or alter the chant.

Like preschoolers, these patients also experiment with rhythmic language, such as "to eat, to eat, to eat, to feet, to feet, to feet." Preschoolers would laugh at this language and add examples to it. But this disorder, known as speech apraxia, is no laughing matter.

Even other Alzheimer's patients find this disorder annoying. Some respond with anger, lashing out with comments like, "If you don't stop saying that I'm going to smack you!" In fact, patients who have speech apraxia are unaware of the condition and have no control over it. Threatening these patients has no effect.

Listeners may imitate involuntary speech in the hope of getting the other person's attention. This doesn't work either. More often than not, other patients shun those who have speech apraxia because the disorder is so disturbing. Even patients who are starting to exhibit signs of speech apraxia will shun these people.

Speech and Personality

When you think about it, a person's speech determines, in part, our perception of them. Much of my perception of my mother comes from her spoken and written words. In the middle of the night, fragments of past conversations seep into my consciousness.

I remember the time Mom saw an elderly woman fall in front of our house. Within seconds, Mom was helping her up, guiding her to a chair on the porch, and giving her a cool drink. Not only do I remember the incident, I remember Mom's advice: "You have to be kind to people."

I remember the words Mom wrote in my sixth grade autograph book: "Trust in the Lord with all your heart and he will direct your path." At times the path has been rough, but I've managed to survive, thanks in part, to Mom's advice and example. Now, failing health and age obscure her personality.

James Mortimer, Ph.D., and coauthors cite the age factor in a research paper in the September 1992 issue of *Neurology*. They say a patient's characteristics can influence the progression of Alzheimer's disease, among them, age at onset, severity, history of alcohol abuse, psychoses, and language impairment.

It seems to me that the smallest speech failure, like saying "book" for "magazine," whittles something away from Mom's personality. I feel like I'm caring for a cardboard cutout, a flat personality lacking depth, subtlety, and judgment. Other caregivers share these feelings.

Repetition

Requests

As Alzheimer's disease gets worse, most patients resort to repetitive speech. Hearing the same sentences day after day and week after week can wear caregivers down. Alzheimer's patients often hone in on a topic to the point of obsession. The topic can be anything—small things like going to the dry cleaner's, finding a nail file, or buying lettuce.

Obsessions can mean extra duty for caregivers. You may go with a patient to buy lettuce, and he or she will ask for more an hour later. Pointing out that you have bought lettuce already upsets the patient. Some patients become so agitated that caregivers give in to keep the peace.

The real issue here is forgetfulness. Alzheimer's patients repeat requests because they've forgotten an idea or fear they will forget it. Each day their minds challenge them to remember and each day they forget something else. Despite the frustration and other emotions this must cause, patients may be reluctant or unable to talk about their feelings.

"Parroting" Conversation

Repeating someone else's sentences, or "parroting," is another form of repetition. Even observant caregivers may be slow to pick up on this symptom. I know it took me a while to realize Mom was losing her ability to create original sentences, parroting mine instead.

For example, when a car cut me off in traffic, I exclaimed, "Look at that driving!" Lost in her own world, Mom didn't notice the car or my exclamation. Several minutes later, though, she suddenly blurted, "Look at that driving!" But the other cars were a mile ahead of us.

Another day I commented, "It's clouding over. I think we'll have rain." After a brief delay, Mom repeated, "It's clouding over. I think we'll have rain." Then she scanned the sky as if checking her own words.

In the dark recesses of her mind, Mom knows our conversations have changed. "You sure talk about the weather a lot," she said. She's right. Bringing up the weather is a way of getting her to talk. Although she can't remember the plots of television programs, she can remember weather forecasts. Unfortunately, many of these forecasts are for other states.

Questions

Alzheimer's patients ask the same questions over and over again. "Caregiving at Home," an Alzheimer's Association brochure, says these questions can exhaust caregivers and points out that they're part of the disease. But knowing this doesn't necessarily make life easier for caregivers.

We can only approach the problem with kindness and compassion. Actually, patients are reassured by our consistent answers to their repeated questions. Our answers may be one of the few constants in their lives. Whether they know it or not, patients are conducting surveys, trying to figure out what has changed and what has stayed the same.

The questions patients ask give us clues to their concerns. My mother has four recurring questions:

1. "Do you remember how old you are?"

2. "Have you got enough money?"

3. "Where did you park the car?"

4. "How do you get in (or out) of here?"

Clearly, dates, finances, transportation, and spatial orientation weigh heavily on Mom's mind. I answer her questions in a reassuring voice and keep my answers short. Mom will ask me these questions again tomorrow.

Storytelling

Caregivers get sick and tired of hearing the same stories. At nearly every Sunday dinner, Mom brings up the topic of my childhood neighborhood. I clench my teeth whenever I hear the lead-in, "Do you remember the old neighborhood?"

This question is followed by a rundown of which family lived in which house. Mom checks off her mental list of neighbors one by one, and I don't interrupt. Her pleasure in telling the story exceeds my displeasure in hearing it. Besides, Mom doesn't talk much any more.

As hard as it is, we must be patient with these stories. Telling stories about the past may be the only conversation the patient can produce. It's better for the patient to use language in this way than not to use it at all. Plus, sharing personal experiences draws caregivers and patients closer together.

Tracking Subjects

Abrupt Changes

Two transmission errors—failure to identify the subject and failure to signal a change of subject—are baffling for caregivers. The Alzheimer's patient may call a caregiver on the phone, abruptly starting a conversation in the middle, without even giving his or her name.

You may feel like Alice in Wonderland, down the rabbit hole, with no clues as to what's going on. "I don't get a 'Hello,' a 'Hi' or anything," one caregiver said. "Suddenly I'm involved in a conversation about going to the mall."

I identified with this comment because Mom has done similar things. We've had many "rabbit hole" conversations. For example, Mom opened one conversation saying, "They're talking now."

"Who's talking?" I asked.

"You know," she countered.

"Who's talking," I persisted.

"The twins. Aren't they talking now?"

Answering questions with questions can get any conversation going in circles. It's difficult for caregivers to track conversations like these, especially if the patient is looking for a specific reply. Giving the "wrong" reply may spark an angry reaction, especially from a patient who is already angry because words aren't coming out as intended.

Generalities and Slang

Many Alzheimer's patients fill conversational voids with generalities. Mom is no exception. Because she couldn't remember the name of her retirement community she began calling it "the big house." Because she couldn't remember the names of other residents, she began calling them "the inmates." To me, these generalities sound like dialogue from a gangster movie.

Gradually "the big house" evolved into "the place," a language change that caused some problems. I discovered "the place" could also mean a grocery store, restaurant, drugstore, whatever. Keeping pace with Mom's changing contexts is a challenge.

Another shift in terminology has occurred. Instead of "the place" Mom now says "our place," an indication, I think, of her increasing dependence on nursing care. "Our place" also expands her sense of family, and she says the words with some ownership. Besides, "our place" sounds more comforting.

Alzheimer's patients also fill conversational voids with slang. This can cause real communication problems because slang is in a state of constant flux. Past slang may differ sharply from present usage. Of course, family and professional caregivers always have the option of asking, "What does that mean?"

Slang adds to the existing confusion and stress that many caregivers feel. Remember, caregivers are already dealing with subject changes, stories, questions, parroting, repetition, speech apraxia, dysarthria, and more. One caregiver admitted, "It's only eight o'clock in the morning, and I'm exhausted."

Time Delays

Searching a mental database for words may cause time delays. It can take Alzheimer's patients minutes, hours, or days to retrieve vocabulary. Aunt Margaret may announce, "You know that word I was trying to think of the other day? Well I thought of it!" Being able to retrieve the word is a matter of pride for Aunt Sadie and others like her.

Be prepared for lapses in conversation and conversation that suddenly "drifts off." The patient may be focused on retrieval or distracted by other events. Or he or she may have simply lost interest in the topic or just be plain sleepy. Caregivers should be aware that slow speech and lack of desire to speak are symptoms of depression. Chapter Four, "Other Causes of Speech Damage," provides more information on this topic.

Time delays are easier to deal with face-to-face because you can follow the patient's visual clues—providing, of course, such clues exist. Dealing with time delays on the phone, especially at long-distance rates, is more difficult. Sometimes it's just easier to change the subject.

Loss of Tact

You may be disturbed by a patient's loss of tact, especially if you're taking care of a failing parent. Loss of tact may be a complete reversal from the mother or father of your childhood. The parent who used to personify tact may become downright blunt.

I was shocked at Mom's loss of tact in the doctor's office. Her doctor, who is one of the kindest, smartest people I've ever met, welcomed her with a ready smile. Mom sat on the edge of the examining table and announced, "Your nose is too large for your face."

The doctor's good nature didn't fail him. "Mabel, you're probably right," he laughed. His agreement silenced her and, thank goodness, she didn't make any more tactless statements. But there have been times when I was forced to ask her to be quiet. Sensitivity disappears when Alzheimer's strikes.

Hurtful Speech

The loss of tact can quickly turn into hurtful speech. I never thought my mother would hurt anyone, but now she says hurtful things all the time. While we were eating lunch at our favorite restaurant Mom said, in a loud voice, "That woman is very masculine."

In a soft voice, which I hoped she would emulate, I replied, "That person is a man."

"She's a man?"

"Yes."

"Then why is he wearing a pink sweater?"

"Maybe he likes pink," I suggested.

"But pink is . . . ."

I put a finger to my lips in a gesture of silence. A crucial fact had escaped Mom's notice. The man at the next table was blind. Could he hear our conversation? "Don't say any more," I said. "Eat your lunch while it's hot."

After we left the restaurant, I told Mom the man she had been talking about was blind. "She's blind?" she asked.

"Yes," I repeated. "He is blind."

"Well, she has a beautiful head of hair."

I failed to see the connection between hair and sight. For a second or two, no more, I thought of explaining things to her again, but I gave up. Our conversation had come full circle, and reviewing the facts wouldn't add to Mom's understanding.

Aggressive Speech

Every caregiver has a story or stories about a patient's aggressive speech. The stories are nearly identical. Some examples:

- "My father told the nurse she was stupid."

- "Yesterday mother called her friend a horse's ass."

- "I never thought my own sister would tell me to go to hell."

- "Dad wrote a letter to a local business owner, threatening to sue him."

- "Can you believe it? My wife thinks I'm having an affair and wants to divorce me."

These beginning sentences usually lead to long explanations, and they are similar, too. However, sharing our feelings with other caregivers is comforting. We're all in this together.

As Mom is drawn deeper into the vortex of Alzheimer's disease, her conversation is peppered with threats. She threatened to kick one person in the shins and smack another in the face. "I'm going to biff her!" Mom shouted. Always a woman of her word, she acted upon these threats.

Family and professional caregivers need to be attuned to aggressive speech. As my mother's behavior proves, aggressive speech can be a preview to actual aggression. We don't want relatives, neighbors, or nursing-home residents living in fear of others. Two simple actions—walking with patients and talking in a calm voice—can soothe agitated patients.

Agreeing with the patient is another helpful tactic. If nothing else, we can agree with their situation. "It's hard to be cooped up in here on a rainy day, isn't it?" Or you may say, "I can understand how you feel. I would feel the same way." These replies validate Alzheimer's patients.

Use of Refrains

Webster's dictionary defines the word *refrain* as "a phrase or verse that recurs regularly." Alzheimer's patients cover up language loss with various refrains. The refrains may be quips from the past, all-purpose replies, such as, "Thanks for everything," or one-word replies, such as, "Right."

Mom uses all three types of refrains. When she's feeling uncertain (as when going for a medical check-up) she plugs in her favorite quip, "I'm A-A-A." Naturally this is followed by the question, "What's that?"

"I'm alive, alert, and alluring!" she exclaims.

Remembering her lines is such a struggle for Mom that she doesn't smile when she says them. However, she expects others to smile or burst into laughter. The first time Mom delivers these lines she does provoke laughter; the second time, the laughter is usually forced.

When she is really groping for words, Mom plugs in the phrase, "all that sort of thing." The phrase is both adaptable and clever. It places responsibility on the listener, who must try to figure out what these things are, while keeping up the conversation.

When confused, she says, "Oh." I didn't know such a short word could be spoken with so many inflections. There's the "Oh!" of surprise, which is said sharply. There's the "Ohhhh" of agreement, which is sustained. There's the questioning "Oh?" which ends on a higher pitch. And there's the don't-you-bring-that-up-again "Oh," firmly stated.

Other caregivers have described similar refrains. While refrains can save the moment, they can't save the day or the week. The day will come when caregivers must confront the truth: The patient's language "tape" is winding down and coming to an end.

Body Language/Gestures

When language starts to fail, body language becomes more important, almost a second language. Alzheimer's patients may point to something they need, such as a sweater, or food they want, such as popcorn. Hundreds of gestures may be used in a week.

In *The 36-Hour Day*, Mace and Rabins encourage caregivers to use body language also. They advise pointing to a body part instead of naming it. After you have pointed to the patient's toe, for example, the patient can indicate whether it hurts or not by nodding. Caregivers have other options as well.

Alzheimer's Association coordinator Bobbie Speich, L.P.N., N.H.A., discussed body language at the Mayo Clinic's first annual conference on Alzheimer's disease, and her points are summarized here:

- Use an open stance and gestures. Don't approach a patient with your hands in your pockets.

- Be cautious about putting your arm around a patient. The patient may think you're trying to restrain him or her and start to struggle.

- Never approach a patient from the rear, which may be interpreted as a threat. However, approaching the patient from an angle may work.

- Mimic the actions you want the patient to take, such as the various steps in brushing and rinsing teeth.

- Make eye contact and look concerned. You want to transmit the message, "I care about you."

• Nod your head while the patient is talking to show you are listening.

Whether it's verbal communication or body language, Speich stressed that caregivers must know their patients. And caregivers must be adaptive. "There will be times when nothing works," she cautioned. At least we get credit for trying.

Some Alzheimer's patients retain the ability to write but can't talk, and vice versa. It's tiring for patients to write their thoughts on paper. We need to encourage these patients and be alert to the signs of fatigue, such as irritability.

Caregivers should also watch for angry gestures and behaviors. When Mom walked by another patient in the hallway one day, the patient grabbed her arm in a claw-like grip. Mom grabbed her back. Despite mutual threats, neither would give in, and staff members had to separate the two.

Intervention is necessary to ensure the safety of all patients. We can only imagine how frustrated someone with Alzheimer's disease must be. It's not unusual for patients to start crying, barge angrily from the room, or shout, "Get away from me!" Wouldn't we do the same?

Changes in speech transmission are only one result of Alzheimer's disease. Over time, patients also experience changes in speech reception. Vision and hearing losses also block communication and the cumulative effect of these factors is devastating. For all we know, Alzheimer's patients are prisoners of their own minds.

CHAPTER 3

Changes in Speech Reception

Topics

What is Agnosia?

Changes in speech reception are a challenge for Alzheimer's patients. Agnosia, or the inability to recognize sensory stimuli, is especially challenging. Experts have divided agnosia into a confusing list of categories and subcategories, each with its own medical name. You don't have to remember these names, but things will be easier for you if you remember this question and answer. For caregivers the crucial question is: What is happening to the patient? For patients the crucial answer is: The familiar is becoming unfamiliar.

Agnosia may involve one, several, or all of the body's senses—vision, hearing, taste, touch, and smell. These impairments confuse Alzheimer's patients; but, more importantly, they give patients false signals. Some common agnosias are:

- Failure to recognize objects (vase, chair, house key, family car, etc.)

- Difficulty recognizing places or spaces (such as the entrance to a grocery store, patient's room in nursing care)

- Reading problems (gradual inability to read, including road signs)

- Inability to perceive color (including shades of the same color and matching color names to objects)

- Unreliable depth perception (for example, not being able to tell where tan carpet ends and a tan wall begins)

Patients in the early stage of Alzheimer's disease may suspect something is wrong but are unable to figure out what that something may be. What can caregivers do? Well, we can keep patients safe, diffuse anger, calm them, and demonstrate caring. A simple smile can transform a patient's day.

Visual Agnosia

Caregivers pick up on visual agnosia—the inability to recognize objects, pictures, and color—very quickly. Although I had read about visual agnosia, I didn't understand it until I recalled two experiences I had with Mom. The first occurred during one of her infamous holiday visits.

Mom took me aside and said she planned to give our younger daughter an afghan for Christmas. "Do you think she would like that?" she asked.

Because she had put so much effort into her Christmas shopping, to the point of physical and mental exhaustion, I wanted to be reassuring. "Well, the temperature has hovered around zero all week," I replied. "An afghan would feel cozy on a winter night."

Mom looked pleased with herself and went to get the afghan. The so-called afghan turned out to be a crocheted rectangle of eye-popping purple, more of a doily than a shawl, and something no college student would ever wear. Should I lie to Mom or tell her the truth?

"That isn't an afghan," I explained. "It's a shawl, you know, something you wear over your shoulders."

Mom's eyes widened in anger. "Then I won't give it to her!" she shouted and threw the shawl across the room. Although the level of her anger was startling, I knew she wasn't angry at me; she was angry at herself, and that's a terrible feeling.

Depth Perception

Visual agnosia includes the inability to perceive changes in height and depth. The patient may stumble on sidewalk curbs or see voids where none exist. "A black and white bathroom floor can look as if it is full of holes," Nancy Mace and Peter Robins explain in *The 36-Hour Day.* These faulty perceptions make patients anxious.

The first inkling I had of Mom's perception problems occurred while we were shopping. I had parked in front of some cement posts. Mom studied the posts with a worried expression on her face and commented, "We'll have to figure out a way to get through there."

"Don't worry, Mom," I answered. "I'll get us through."

"Good," she replied.

But everything about her body language—her stiffness, facial expression, tight grip on my arm—revealed her concern. In her mind, the posts were as obstructive as the Berlin Wall; they entrapped her and kept her from reaching her destination. "If we get through, how will we get back?" she asked.

Nursing homes and adult day-care centers are using depth perception problems like these to help patients. Someone discovered that Alzheimer's patients will stop and turn around when they encounter fringe. So many facilities have installed beaded and plastic fringe in selected doorways. The result? Fewer Alzheimer's patients have been found wandering.

Sticking tape to the floor in parallel lines has a similar effect. These safety measures, along with installing musical alarms on exit doors, help staff members to do their jobs more efficiently. Still these gimmicks are not a replacement for competent care.

Differentiation

A patient who has agnosia may not be able to tell the difference between a large bottle of ketchup and a small one. Or the patient may be unable to see a rose bush in the middle of a garden. Like other Alzheimer's patients, Mom has lots of differentiation problems.

I had moved her four times, and each time I tried to make her apartment attractive and tidy. Because she had been having trouble coordinating outfits, I grouped her wardrobe by color: black blouses with matching skirts and slacks, black shoes with black boots, etc. It turned out that I had done Mom a terrible disservice.

She decided her black boots had been stolen. I could not imagine who would want her old boots and said so. However, Mom insisted I come over and "take action." The boots were in the left-hand corner of the closet, exactly where I had put them. "Here they are," I said.

Peeking around the closet door, Mom blinked in disbelief. "Oh," she said, dismissing the crisis in an instant.

Instead of putting the boots back where they had been, I put them by the closet door where she would see them. You can guess what happened. Those boots disappeared again. Asking Mom to find black boots in a crowded closet was asking her to do the impossible.

Word Blindness

Depending on the neurological pathways that are involved, word blindness may be classified as an agnosia or an aphasia. Patients with word blindness may be able to write and spell but unable to read.

The note you leave on a refrigerator door may be misread or ignored. Seemingly obvious clues, such as an arrow or a stop sign, are ignored as well.

According to *Principles of Neurology*, word blindness is often discovered by accident. If you observe the patient closely, you can get an idea of the extent of their word blindness. Usually word blindness happens slowly over time. Look for a diminished interest in reading, poor comprehension, and books and articles that are started but never finished. As one patient volunteered, "I don't like to read much any more." This same patient thought the lettering on a box was upside down, when in fact, the lettering was right-side up. While large-print books keep patients interested in reading for a while, their interest gradually wanes. However, many patients are able to enjoy books on tape and to follow a story that is read aloud to them.

Vision Loss

Patients who have visual agnosia may have actual vision loss. As we get older our eyes don't accommodate light changes as easily, and few of us can read small print without glasses. More crucial for the Alzheimer's patient is the fact that vision can change quickly.

Even if the patient's eyes were checked recently, a recheck is a good idea. While he or she is examining the patient's eyes, the ophthalmologist will look for glaucoma, cataracts, and retina problems.

Caregivers can help by putting a chain or ribbon on glasses so they won't get lost. We can also clean glasses regularly. Wearing glasses spotted with fingerprints and food is almost as dangerous as not wearing glasses at all—an accident waiting to happen. You might want to provide a special case or box for glasses, too.

Auditory Agnosia

The inability to differentiate words and environmental sounds is called auditory agnosia. This reception error may start with the complaint, "Talk louder. I can't hear you." But talking louder doesn't help an impaired mind to process sound accurately.

Auditory agnosia can actually be life-threatening, or at the very least, put the patient in harm's way. Steven Rapesak, M.D., and his colleagues discuss this reception problem in their research paper, "Impaired Recognition of Meaningful Sounds in Alzheimer's Disease." The study compared 18 patients with senile dementia of the Alzheimer's type (SDAT) with a control group.

Subjects were given hearing evaluations, sound-recognition tests, picture-recognition tests, and language tests. "A significant impairment of sound recognition was found in the SDAT group, consistent with auditory sound agnosia," notes the paper. The authors believe their research warrants dividing SDAT patients into perceptual-discriminative and semantic-associative types.

Without going into too much detail, the research paper says the inability to recognize incoming sound is "a significant liability for patients." For example, the patient may not be able to hear a car horn. Therefore, the authors recommend additional warning signs on smoke alarms, telephones, and doorbells.

Mom developed a curious auditory agnosia. Since she didn't know anyone in town, she often called to ask, "What are you doing?" I would give her a rundown on my plans for the day. No matter how loudly I spoke—so loud I became hoarse—Mom couldn't hear me.

"I can't hear on this damn thing!" she exclaimed. "You will have to buy me a new phone."

Our phone conversations got progressively worse, and Mom's replies were reduced to a curt, "Huh?" Things got curiouser and curiouser. The phone would ring, I would answer it and then hear fumbling noises and a disconnect. I received three calls one week and five the next. Was someone trying to harass me?

Before I contacted the phone company, I acted upon a hunch. Immediately after the disconnect, I called my mother. "Oh, I just called but you were out," she complained.

"No, I was here, Mom," I said.

"You were not. You were out," she insisted. "I keep trying to call you and you're always out."

Clearly, Mom's brain interpreted a phone connection as a disconnection. Our primary means of communication no longer worked. Then Mom lost the ability to recognize my voice on the phone. Whenever I called, she would answer, listen for a second, and reply in dulcet tones, "You have the wrong number. Please hang up and call again."

Mom sounded so professional I wondered how many wrong numbers she had dialed to attain this skill. It was time for a new plan. I started relaying messages through staff members. As you might expect, this did not work very well, and turned into a real-life version of the "telephone game."

I tried, without success, to explain Mom's phone problems to her. "You have trouble hearing me on the phone," I began.

"I don't talk to you because you're never home," she accused. "Yesterday I called, and you weren't home."

"I was home all day," I said.

"No you weren't," she insisted. "The man who answered said 'Harriet isn't here.'"

"Was it John?"

"No, but the man said 'Harriet isn't here,'" she repeated.

Mom's phone problems continued, and several months later I cancelled her service. There was no point in paying for something we couldn't use. However, I asked the staff to leave the phone on the nightstand next to Mom's bed. Having a phone close at hand makes her feel secure.

Hearing Loss

Keep in mind that someone with Alzheimer's disease may have auditory agnosia and a hearing loss. Two early symptoms of hearing loss are missing conversation or adding strange comments to a conversation. The patient may also complain about ringing in the ears (tinnitus) and each ear may hear a different tone.

Some patients describe tinnitus as roaring or hissing sounds. The patient should have a professional hearing exam to rule out hearing loss. But be forewarned: Detecting hearing loss in Alzheimer's patients is a challenge for the most skillful examiner.

Testing For Hearing Loss

Audiologists are confronted with a number of problems when someone with Alzheimer's disease walks in the door. First, the patient's brain may be slow to discern sounds, the basis of the entire exam. Second, he or she may forget to push the response button, which shows up as a hearing loss on paper.

Third, it's difficult for someone with Alzheimer's to concentrate on the task. His or her mind may wander, or the patient may have an overwhelming desire to sleep. Finally, the various sounds in the hearing test—random stimuli—may generate random responses. These responses skew the test.

Mom's test showed sufficient hearing loss to warrant a hearing aid. As I discovered, buying a hearing aid for someone with Alzheimer's doesn't necessarily help them. And matching a hearing aid to the patient's audiogram can also be difficult, especially in cases of high-frequency loss.

Hearing Aids

Great strides have been made in hearing aid technology. The batteries are more efficient, and the hearing aids have gotten smaller. Mom was fitted with a hearing aid and allowed to try it for several months. At first she was delighted with it, but then she lost her ability to operate it.

She couldn't remember that turning the dial forward made sounds louder and turning the dial backward made sounds softer. She kept leaving the hearing aid on at night, which drained batteries at a prodigious rate. Hearing aids have to be cleaned with a tiny wire, but Mom couldn't do that either.

We were living in Stillwater, Minnesota, at the time so I arranged for batteries to be delivered and the hearing aid to be cleaned. Mom kept losing the $850 hearing aid (now worth far more), and staff members couldn't find it. "If your hearing aid is gone, we won't get another," I said angrily.

The minute the words were out of my mouth, I was ashamed. I couldn't believe I had said something so unkind to my mother. A week later she found her hearing aid beneath some underwear in her chest of drawers. But because she rarely remembers how to work it, the discovery did her little good.

Misidentification

In the final stage of Alzheimer's, patients no longer recognize themselves in a mirror. The patient may ask, "Who is that?" This misidentification and others are discussed in an article by Alistair Burns and his colleagues, which appeared in the *British Journal of Psychiatry*. Burns and his colleagues cite the following as examples of visual and auditory hallucinations.

- *People in the house.* This is a common misidentification in Alzheimer's patients. The patient may think a gang has moved into the house. To make matters worse, some patients confuse misidentifications with dreams.

- *Misidentification of mirror image.* The patient may look into the mirror and see a stranger's face. One father asked his daughter why the person in the mirror was "so grouchy."

- *Misidentification of television.* With this syndrome, the patient talks to the television set or believes all of the events on the screen are real. Both of these misidentifications magnify the patient's fears.

- *Misidentification of people.* This agnosia is painful for family members. One nursing home resident doesn't always recognize his wife, although she shares his room. Curiously, he recognizes her when she is in the hallway, the television room, or the dining room.

Like repetitive questions, misidentifications can mean extra duty for caregivers. When things get stressful, we need to practice self-care and take a few hours off. This is easier said than done, I know, but it's necessary if we're going to survive the caregiving process.

Coming to False Conclusions

Reception changes cause many patients to come to false conclusions. One man made a false conclusion about laundry. The retirement community he lived in had set up a weekly schedule to avoid overcrowding in the laundry room, and this man did his laundry on the wrong day.

When other residents pointed this out to him, the man became furious. Anger contributed to his false conclusion: I am not allowed to use the laundry equipment.

"Well, I showed them a thing or two," he declared later. "I did my laundry anyway and told them to go to hell!"

One of Mom's false conclusions turned out to be painful for both of us. Early one morning she called and asked, "Am I going back to Long Island today?" My mind was racing at top speed, trying to figure out how I would answer this question without hurting her feelings.

"No," I answered, still trying to think.

"Well, when am I going?" she asked.

"You're not," I said bluntly. "You live here now."

"I live here?"

"Yes."

"Well, that's news to me!" she said angrily.

I could tell Mom was revving up for a good argument, so I changed the subject. But the conversation surprised me so, I jotted it down on paper—and I'm glad I did. As time elapsed, my mother's memory of the conversation became distorted. Whenever she can, wherever she can, she tells her version of the story:

"Do you know what my daughter told me? She told me I better get used to this place because it's my home. Can you imagine her saying that? I better get used to this place? Well, I hate it here. I hate it! I hate it!"

Implied here is the false conclusion that I don't care about my mother. Her conclusion has made my caretaking more difficult. To make matters worse, Mom feels superior to everyone else in nursing care. "There are a lot of crazy people here," she confides in a whisper. "I try to straighten them out."

When Are They Coming?

Alzheimer's patients often convince themselves that a family member is coming to visit. In short, their minds turn fantasy into reality. Take the case of Gladys, a woman in her mid-70s. Gladys had an apartment in an assisted-living facility and lived there under close supervision. Every morning, she went to the main door of the apartment building to watch for her daughter.

"My daughter is coming from Seattle to visit me," Gladys said confidently. "She'll be here at noon."

Unfortunately this wasn't true. The staff worried about Gladys because she kept stepping in front of the electronic doors and had a tendency to wander. Gladys could be lured away from the door with a snack or an activity, but the next morning she went to the door again. "She does this every day," a staff member explained.

Once an Alzheimer's patient has made up his or her mind, you probably won't be able to change it. One false conclusion leads to another. The son who can't visit may be accused of not loving a parent or absconding with the family funds. Actually, job and family responsibilities, lack of funds, and health problems may keep the son from visiting more often.

This is a no-win situation for caregivers. The mental impairments caused by Alzheimer's disease keep patients from understanding cause-effect relationships or remembering them. Because we can't change the disease, we might as well accept the situation and move on.

Sexual Fantasies

Those of us who are caring for failing parents may be shocked by their sexuality. Maybe our shock stems from the cultural myth that sex is reserved for the young. Older people—especially the grandparents of our children—aren't supposed to have sexual feelings. Something must be wrong with them. In truth, sexuality transcends age.

I was surprised when Mom referred to another resident of nursing care as her boyfriend. It's impossible to tell if she meant this in a sexual or a platonic way. Perhaps "boyfriend" is 1930s slang. All I know is Mom believes several men are interested in her, and she asked one to take her dancing.

Some Alzheimer's patients develop hypersexual agitation—inappropriate and excessive sexual behaviors. According to Carl F. Jensen, M.D., of University of Washington in Seattle, examples of hypersexual agitation include verbal comments, hugging, kissing, self-exposure, and attempted fondling. In a letter to the American Geriatrics Society, Dr. Jensen points out that hypersexual agitation can be a form of aggression.

I think sexual fantasies are also a cry for affection, a need all humans share. Some years ago my mother and father-in-law visited a friend in a nursing home. At the conclusion of the visit they hugged their friend. "Oh, that feels good," she said. "I haven't been hugged in years."

My mother-in-law never forgot the comment. Thinking about the visit always brought tears to her eyes. There must be thousands of Alzheimer's patients who yearn for affection. Alzheimer's disease causes memory problems, but the memory of a hug is often retained. So let's be generous with our hugs. Someday we may be yearning for affection.

"Random" I.Q.

Just when you think you understand Alzheimer's, it turns around and fools you. After months of passive behavior, the patient may wake up and become lucid. This takes family and professional caregivers by surprise. You wouldn't be the first caregiver to ask yourself, "Did I miss something?"

It's easier to understand Alzheimer's if you think of the patient's mind as a damaged computer diskette. Parts of the diskette are perfect, and parts are damaged. What's more, things can change in an instant—as I found out.

Mom had been unresponsive for months, nonverbal, unsmiling, and lost in her own world. One Sunday evening, she brightened up and started asking questions. "Have you seen the twins?" "How are my stocks doing?" "What are you writing now?" "Where's my winter coat?"

Caregivers are constantly adapting and readapting to the patient's intelligence. Months after I had cancelled her phone service, Mom asked a nurse to dial our number, and talked intelligently on the phone. Once she recognized my voice, which took a moment, she got straight to the point: "I want a banana."

This request brought a smile to my face because we had talked about bananas a week ago. If there's anything Mom misses on her diabetic diet, it's desserts, and she eyes them longingly. "I can't eat desserts, so they give me lots of bananas at the place," she said. "I've eaten so many it's a wonder I don't look like a banana!"

I burst out laughing. "Well, Mom, if you start to look like a banana, I'll tell you," I replied.

The spark in Mom's voice was heartwarming. This was the mother of my childhood, the funny person who made others laugh and who laughed at herself as well. Much to my surprise, Mom continued the conversation later in the car. "If I looked like a banana, I'd have yellow hair and skin," she said.

"Yes," I agreed. "Anyway, bananas are good for you, so keep eating them."

"That's probably why I'm so beautiful at age 90," she joked.

"You look great, Mom," I said, patting her hand. "I promise to tell you if you start looking like a banana, and you can do the same for me."

Rare moments of intelligence like these are a gift. I'm gathering a mental bouquet of these moments and hope they will sustain me in the future. But I know these moments are becoming scarcer and will be gone soon. Therefore, I cherish each one and clutch it to my heart.

Individual Differences

While patients with Alzheimer's have similar symptoms, there are many individual differences among patients. Some experts think the disease magnifies personality traits. "My mother was always a sweet person," a friend told me. "Now that she has Alzheimer's, she's sweeter than ever." Of course, the reverse may also be true.

Does Alzheimer's alter the patient's personality? Fernando G. Bozzola, M.D., and his colleagues discuss this question in their paper, "Personality Changes in Alzheimer's Disease." Caregivers notice personality changes quickly, they say, and this adds to their burdens. According to the researchers, the most common personality changes are apathy, diminished interest in hobbies, and a rigid personality.

The role of caregiver is an expanding one. The more the patient fails, the more we must do for them. Simple errands, such as grocery shopping with the patient, take twice or three times as long. Trying to rush the patient with actions or words is futile.

Each change in reception is a communication blocker. But many other factors contribute to the breakdown of language. The next chapter discusses these physical and psychological factors, not the least of which is going into a nursing home. How did life come to this?

CHAPTER 4

Other Causes of Speech Deterioration

Topics

Multiple Illnesses

Nervous Tics and Mannerisms

Medications

Pain

Poor Oral Hygiene

Depression

Suicidal Thoughts

"Sundowning"

Psychoses

Going to a Nursing Home

Hidden Messages

Violent Behavior

We could say the odds are stacked against patients because most of them have other illnesses besides Alzheimer's disease. Communication between patients and caregivers is altered by these illnesses and the medications used to treat them. Let's examine the effects of multiple illnesses on speech.

Multiple Illnesses

Some illnesses, such as stroke, affect speech directly and profoundly. But other illnesses, such as diabetes, contribute to speech deterioration in more subtle ways. The patient's speech may be altered by:

- Malnutrition, which can impair thinking

- Dehydration, resulting in confused thinking and speech

- High blood pressure

- Fatigue, making the patient too tired to speak

- Hypothyroidism, which can slow speech

- Emphysema (patient may gasp for breath or have coughing spells)

- Rotting or missing teeth, which cause bad breath and articulation problems

- Infections or fever, resulting in confused thinking and speech

- Incontinence, (patient may stop talking suddenly and complain of discomfort)

- Diabetes, resulting in confused thinking and slower speech

- Depression, which may inhibit or stop speech

- Migraine headaches, resulting in confused thinking and speech

- Other neurological diseases.

Dehydration

Dehydration is a common health problem for Alzheimer's patients. They may not drink enough liquid or rely on caffeinated beverages for hydration. Experts advise cutting down on caffeine because it is a diuretic. So caregivers need to be aware of the type and amount of beverages the patient consumes.

Of course the best thirst quencher is water. You might want to stock the patient's refrigerator with plain water (in a bottle or pitcher), flavored waters, iced herbal tea, and juices. Patients with digestive problems may prefer low-acid juices, such as apple or grape juice.

Diet

Too many elderly people eat a diet that is high in starches and low in fruits and vegetables. Jo Horne, author of *Caregiving: Helping an Aging Loved One*, attributes poor diet to a diminished sense of taste, the effort of cooking, poor eyesight, loneliness (eating alone isn't fun), and money problems. "When money is tight, unfortunately many older people will sacrifice a balanced diet in favor of meals that are cheap and filling," she explains.

My mother seemed to be eating a well-balanced diet but started to complain of thirst. Her diabetes was discovered during a routine physical exam. At first, her diabetes could be controlled by diet, but she quickly forgot she had the disease.

Not only did she eat sweets, she binged on cookies and pastries, devouring an entire peach pie in a matter of hours. To help her make better food choices, the staff put up reminder notes and a healthy snacks poster. Mom ignored the notes and thought the poster was a colorful decoration.

Another factor, unknown to me at the time, also affected Mom's diabetes. It turns out that she was eating double meals. She would forget I had taken her to lunch and order another lunch from the dining room an hour later. Eating double meals didn't help her diabetes.

If Mom continued to binge on sweets, she could go into a diabetic coma. Things got so bad the nursing staff had to raid her apartment. "People have been stealing my cookies and pastries!" Mom exclaimed. "They're mine, and I want them back!"

When I reminded her about her diabetes she looked at me in utter disbelief. I arranged for Mom to eat all of her meals in the dining room. The dietitian said the staff would monitor her intake as carefully as possible. But nobody could watch her every minute.

Mom's diabetes got bad enough to warrant insulin. In fact, her insulin dosage has been increased three times. Still, regular blood checks and insulin shots don't help her remember her diabetes. "They keep pricking my finger and giving me shots," Mom complained. "I wonder why they do that?"

Nervous Tics and Mannerisms

Many Alzheimer's patients have nervous tics and mannerisms. Tongue-thrusting is a particularly unpleasant mannerism for observers. Other mannerisms, such as humming, throat-clearing, and yawning are just plain irritating.

My mother has so many mannerisms, it's a wonder we converse at all. Her head bobs constantly, she slaps her knee with one hand, rubs her eyebrow, and makes purring noises in her throat. The purring can get so loud and rhythmic it sounds like a coffee pot. In addition, she taps her feet in a series of three. My mind interprets the tap-tap-tap as "Hur-ry up!"

And Mom's hearing aid squeaks constantly. Listeners are distracted by the sound, although Mom seems oblivious to it. Between the foot-tapping, throat-purring, eyebrow-rubbing, hand-slapping, and head-bobbing, our communication is poor at best.

Medications

Medications can react unfavorably with each other, react with other foods, such as milk, or have a cumulative affect on the patient. As a caregiver, it's important that you know all medications the patient is taking and how they might interact. Your pharmacist is an excellent resource if you need information.

Mom's medications were delivered to her apartment, each in a separate, labeled envelope. For a while, she could be relied upon to take her medications. However, the nursing staff eventually began to suspect she was skipping doses. They searched her apartment and found 18 envelopes of pills.

My only recourse was to increase support services, which, in turn, increased her monthly bill. The time had come to keep better track of her medications. I talked with her pharmacist and listed Mom's medications in my address file. You might want to keep a formal medications log in a notebook.

Reactions to Medication

Different Alzheimer's patients may react to the same medication in very different ways. Finding the appropriate medication for a patient can be a slow process. "Every time we thought we had found the right medication it would have damaging side effects on Dad," one caregiver recalled. "Then we'd have to start all over again."

The medications that cause drowsiness put a damper on conversation. Your best conversational efforts may be greeted with silence. That's OK. Silence can be a welcome change of pace in our busy, noisy lives. We can respect the patient's need for silence and solitude.

Overmedicating

Alzheimer's patients are very sensitive to medication. In the past, it was common for nursing homes to over-medicate patients to control agitation and help them sleep. This practice has been discontinued (with some exceptions), but some patients accidentally overmed-icate themselves.

Mildred was an 85-year-old widow who lived alone. While rummaging through her kitchen drawers, she found a bottle of antibiotics prescribed two years ago for a bladder infection. Although Mildred didn't have a bladder infection, she resumed taking the antibiotics.

As it turned out, however, antibiotics weren't the only medication Mildred was taking improperly.

The last time Mildred's son talked with her on the phone, she sounded so sleepy and confused he became alarmed. He became more alarmed after he examined the contents of his mother's medicine cabinet. It seemed Mildred was taking a fistful of pills at lunchtime, analgesics to help her sleep at night, vita-mins in the morning to pep her up, antacids through-out the day, and occasional sleeping pills. No wonder Mildred was sleepy and confused.

If you think a loved one is overmedicated, contact his or her doctor. Questions that need answering include:

1. How many prescription medications is the patient taking?

2. How many nonprescription medications is the patient taking?

3. What are the side effects of these medications?

4. Are all of the medications necessary?

5. Can any dosages be lowered?

After reviewing the case, you may find that some medications can be discontinued. To be on the safe side, caregivers should remove expired and unlabeled medicine from the patient's home. Also, dispose of unnecessary over-the-counter medications. Having a "larder" of pills is trouble waiting to happen.

Pain

Potential sources of pain for Alzheimer's patients, as for other older adults, are numerous. Among them are stomach cramps, constipation, sprains, being in the same position too long, arthritis, pressure sores, scratches and bruises, sore teeth and gums, and poorly fitting dentures and shoes. Alzheimer's patients express their pain by moaning, shouting, refusing to cooperate, restless behavior, or silence.

Dee Carlson, M.A., L.S.W. of the Mayo Clinic observed, "People with Alzheimer's disease don't tend to talk about pain." Certainly, pain can bring communication to an abrupt halt. Patients who are in severe pain may curl into the fetal position and withdraw into themselves. We shouldn't assume the patient is out of touch, however.

Just because the patient is silent doesn't mean he or she isn't listening to our conversation. We need to be careful about what we say. Never discuss the patient in his or her presence or resort to baby talk. Instead, use simple words, short sentences, and speak on an adult level.

We can also help the patient by investigating their pain. Ask as many "yes" or "no" questions as possible. Try to pinpoint the location and type of pain (steady, throbbing, increasing, decreasing, etc.). Moderate the pitch of your voice and assure the patient that help is on the way.

These days there is no reason for an Alzheimer's patient to be in constant pain. Great strides have been made in drug therapy and pain management. Chances are the doctor will be able to relieve much of the patient's pain. In theory, this should improve communication, but there are no guarantees.

Poor Oral Hygiene

Dentists know Alzheimer's patients often have poor oral hygiene. Painful dentures, missing teeth, and bad breath all inhibit speech. You might want to arrange for staff members to brush the patient's teeth. The dentist can prescribe a special toothpaste to inhibit decay.

Cleaning teeth poses a number of challenges for many patients, not the least of which is finding the toothbrush. The Alzheimer's Association says brushing involves 32 separate steps. Patients will be more successful if caregivers break down the task into a series of small steps. Caregivers should also mimic the actions they are seeking—opening the tube, squeezing paste onto the brush, and so on.

Rotting teeth and infected roots must be removed from the patient's mouth. Because general anesthesia could impair the patient's remaining memory, a local anesthetic is usually recommended. After the surgery, the patient might want to take an analgesic for pain.

Alzheimer's patients often lose their dentures and they could be anywhere—under the bed, under a plate, in a pocket, or heaven forbid, in the trash. Without teeth, the patient's speech may be sloppy or unintelligible. Dentures should be stored in a plastic denture box labeled with the patient's name. Some nursing homes keep dentures in a central place overnight to prevent loss.

Depression

David Carroll, author of *When Your Loved One Has Alzheimer's*, says it's difficult to differentiate depression from Alzheimer's disease. "It is estimated that before 1982, one-third of patients diagnosed as having Alzheimer's disease were actually suffering from depression," observes Carroll.

But many Alzheimer's patients have genuine depression, a response, in part, to change. W. Walter Menninger, M.D., writes about change in the *Menninger Perspective*. While each stage of life contains change, our later years are filled with intense changes. "It is not always possible to anticipate or schedule periods of significant change," Dr. Menninger writes.

When change is unexpected, the response is often low morale. Who wouldn't have low morale? Many patients are reeling from a series of crises—the death of a spouse, forced relocation, dwindling funds, the death of friends, not to mention news headlines.

Acutely depressed patients may develop a "flat affect." If you ask the patient how he or she is feeling, you may get a lethargic, "I . . . feel . . . just. . . fine." Of course, you know the patient is far from fine.

Unfortunately, family and professional caregivers may disagree on how the patient's depression should be treated. Take the case of Walter, a grandfather in his mid-80s. Two weeks after Walter moved into a nursing home, he became depressed. A psychiatrist was consulted and, to the dismay of relatives, recommended shock treatments and cognitive therapy. It's true that shock therapy may help senile depression, but the family opposed these recommendations for two reasons.

First, shock treatments would further confuse a confused patient. Second, the patient didn't have the mental skills that cognitive therapy required. After several weeks of arguing, the family caregivers prevailed. Because the patient was already taking six prescription medications and near death, family members vetoed the use of antidepressants.

However, some Alzheimer's patients are helped by anti-depressants. These drugs must be prescribed by a doctor, and the side effects should be monitored carefully. We shouldn't expect miracles, though. The antidepressant may lift the patient's general mood, but it probably won't erase their depression completely.

Suicidal Thoughts

Society's response to Alzheimer's patients sends them a clear—albeit unwritten—message. According to Deborah Shelton Pinkney, in an article in *American Medical News*, the message is: "If you're depressed and thinking about suicide, good for you."

In other words, these are disposable people.

All too often, depression isn't recognized in Alzheimer's patients. Either the caregivers don't know the symptoms or they discount them. And shocking as it is, some elderly people commit suicide to retain their dignity. Committing suicide is a way of having some control over an uncontrollable life.

Experts are starting to pay more attention to elderly suicide, but the problem has largely been ignored. Why? "There's a stigma among the older adult population about going to mental health services," says Sharon Autio, interim codirector of Minnesota's Mental Health Division.

Then too, some health professionals, especially the younger ones, are reluctant to take care of the elderly.

I'm not a doctor, but I could tell Mom was acutely depressed the Christmas after my father died. When I met her at the airport, she was dressed completely in black and her face was expressionless. During the intervening years Mom's depression has gotten worse. She has threatened to commit suicide by jumping from the eighth-floor window or taking a bottle of pills.

All suicide threats should be taken seriously. More than a cry for help, a suicide threat is a cry from the soul. Family and professional caregivers must also be aware of the role loneliness plays in depression. Patients who are involved—who have a reason to get up in the morning—are less likely to become depressed.

Caregiver's Response

While caregivers are trying to keep Alzheimer's patients alive, the patients may feel they have outlived their usefulness. At least that's the way it is with Mom. "I never thought I would live this long," she said. "I haven't had a very happy life."

"Well, John and I are glad you've lived so long," I replied. "You've lived long enough to see John's career progress, my books get published, and your twin great-grandchildren. That's a lot to be happy about."

"You may see it that way, but I don't," Mom snapped. "There isn't much to be happy about."

As I discovered, caregivers can't imprint their ideas on Alzheimer's patients. We don't know what's going on in their minds. One resident of a nursing home suddenly burst into tears. The nurse rushed over to the patient, knelt down in front of her, and grasped her hands.

"You're all so kind to me, but I want to cry," the patient said. "I don't know what's wrong with me."

"Go ahead and cry," the nurse replied. "We understand." The nurse paused for a few moment. "Sometimes crying makes you feel better, so go ahead and cry."

The patient started to cry harder. "The memories build up . . . I just want to cry . . . I just want to meet my maker," she sobbed.

Several minutes later the patient's tears had subsided, thanks in part to the nurse's response. The nurse had validated the patient's feelings. Despite their mental impairments, Alzheimer's patients come to terms with the fact that death is part of life. We must do the same.

"Sundowning"

Sooner or later caregivers become familiar with "sundowning," popularly defined as late afternoon wandering or pacing. Michael Vitiello, Ph.D., and his co-researchers at the University of Washington in Seattle define sundowning as delirium during evening and nighttime hours and say sleep disturbances contribute to it.

About 40 percent of the time a patient is in bed at night, he or she is awake, and many daytime hours are spent sleeping. This disturbance in the sleep/wake cycle throws off the patient's circadian rhythm. The common features of sundowning include an inability to track events, disorganized thinking and speech, restless or agitated behaviors, perceptual disturbances (such as delusions or hallucinations) and emotional problems.

Despite the development of coping strategies, some researchers think more study is needed before we understand sundowning and how to respond to it. Although tolerance is a relative thing, most family caregivers can't tolerate the night wandering that accompanies sundowning.

Caregivers may lie awake half the night, listening for sounds, and wondering what the patient will do next. Needless to say, this is stressful on caregivers, who often wind up in sleep deprivation. Sundowning is one of the primary reasons for transferring patients to nursing homes. However, moving the patient into a nursing home adds to their confusion. Alzheimer's patients may become psychotic and lose touch with reality.

Psychoses

Medical dictionaries define psychosis as a mental disorder characterized by disintegration of the patient's personality. According to researcher George S. Zubenko, M.D., Ph.D., and colleagues, longitudinal studies suggest that 50 percent of Alzheimer's patients suffer from psychosis by the time of death.

Writing in the *American Journal of Psychiatry,* Dr. Zubenko and his colleagues report that short-term hospitalization has been effective in treating these patients and may help keep them out of institutions. "It may also reduce the need for institutionalization," they say.

Hallucinations

Whether they're in a hospital or at home, many Alzheimer's patients have hallucinations. These are very real to patients. One night, my mother awoke to a disturbing hallucination. "When I woke up, there were people standing around my bed," she began. "They all wanted to live in my apartment. It took me a while to figure out the people weren't real and that I was dreaming. Wasn't that a silly thing to do?"

Since I couldn't think of a reply, I agreed with her. I doubt that Mom could separate hallucinations from dreams today. Hallucinations frighten both caregivers and patients. The patient doesn't know what is going on, and the caregiver may think the patient is mentally ill.

Don't assume that Alzheimer's disease is causing the hallucinations. Medications, fever, or other diseases may be the cause. Comfort the patient as best you can, and contact the patient's doctor. You may also want to consult a geriatric specialist.

Delusions

Delusions are false beliefs that persist contrary to evidence. Thinking a doll is a real baby is an innocent-enough delusion. The patient may cuddle the doll and talk to it like she used to talk to her own children. But thinking car headlights are giant fireballs is a terrifying delusion.

In fact, delusions can be so terrifying that patients scream, push, and hit caregivers in self-defense. We can only imagine the terrors a patient is experiencing. Experts say you shouldn't argue with a patient about their delusions, just accept them.

Nevertheless, our replies can be honest. "I'm not sure what you're talking about, but it sounds scary." "I'm sure you were frightened. Are you feeling better now?" "I've never experienced anything like that, but I believe you." Comments like these validate the patient.

Going to a Nursing Home

Putting a loved one in a nursing home is a trauma for all concerned. These days, the decision to place a loved one in a nursing home is usually made by consensus. Family members, friends, social workers, staff members, and health professionals help make the decision.

Individual states have passed laws to help impaired patients. For example, the state of Minnesota requires a doctor's examination within 10 days of admittance to nursing care. The law also requires regular care conferences and inspection of nursing homes. Like many other caregivers, I find these regulations comforting and am relieved my mother is in a safe place.

"Not Me" Thinking

Mom decided she was in nursing care by mistake and would be returning to her apartment soon. This kind of "not me" thinking complicates things for family caregivers. Once Mom realized she wasn't returning to her apartment, she became volatile.

The smallest incident would set her off. Nothing was right—food, clothing, schedule, caregiving—and nothing could be made right. I walked into nursing care one day and discovered Mom was in the throes of a good, old-fashioned tantrum. "I hate it here, and I don't belong here!" She yelled.

"You're just where you need to be, Mom," I replied, consciously keeping my voice low and calm.

"Why?"

"You have had at least five small strokes, you have diabetes, and you have a metal socket in your shoulder. You're here because you need lots of medical help."

Mom wasn't about to give up and started the script again. "Well, I don't belong here."

"I'm not going to talk about it any more," I said firmly. "It's time to go to the dentist." Changing the subject slowed her down a bit, but she resumed her tirade in the car. These outbursts frighten me, and I think Mom is frightened also. Out-of-control feelings are always frightening.

Behavioral Disturbances

Behavorial disturbances alter speech and body language. Researchers Timothy Lukovits and Keith McDaniel, M.D., identified 12 specific behavioral disturbances in Alzheimer's patients living in nursing homes. For study purposes the researchers divided behavioral disturbances into three categories:

1. Psychological disturbances—depression, fears, paranoia, delusions, hallucinations, and disinterest

2. Activity disturbances—agitation, wandering, and repeating

3. Vegetative disturbances—dietary change, sleep disturbances, and incontinence

Family and professional caregivers answered a questionnaire about the disturbances. Results of the cross-sectional study were reported in the *Journal of the American Geriatrics Society*. Both family and professional caregivers agreed there were fewer disturbances in the last stage of Alzheimer's. Nurses were more upset about vegetative disturbances than were family members, however, probably because they were primary caregivers.

Improving Communication

Can nursing home patients improve their communication? Two nurses, Rita Friedman, Ph.D., and Ruth Tappen, Ed.D., asked themselves this question. They conducted an experimental study of 30 patients in two nursing homes. Their results were reported in the *Journal of the American Geriatrics Society.*

Both groups were given the same communications test. The people in one group walked individually for 30 minutes, three times a week, over a course of 10 weeks. The people in the other group spent this time conversing about topics relevant to their lives.

Members of the walking group scored higher on the communication retests than the nonwalking group.

"The results suggest that a planned walking program has the capacity to improve the communication performance of patients with Alzheimer's disease," the researchers concluded.

I suspect that any type of exercise—throwing a ball or stretching—would help patients. Even though the patient doesn't exercise very long, the exercise stimulates body and mind. If nothing else, the patients can talk about exercise.

Hidden Messages

Because Alzheimer's kills brain cells, patients may say one thing and mean another. In order to "hear" these hidden messages we must know the patient and factor in his or her life experience. What is the patient really saying?

Statement:
"I hate this place."

Hidden Message:
"I miss my things, and don't like living with strangers."

Statement:
"You're talking to the Vice President of the Resident Council."

Hidden Message:
"I need to be needed."

Statement:
"Everyone is crazy."

Hidden Message:
"I see people doing odd things and wonder if I am doing them, too."

Statement:
"They take good care of me here."

Hidden Message:
"I like feeling protected and safe."

Statement:
"I let my son do things for me, like managing my funds."

Hidden Message:
"Giving my son permission to do things makes me feel more in control."

Although the patient's messages may be hidden, ours must be visible and clear. We need to tell patients we have their welfare at heart, reinforcing this message with action and praising them for their efforts.

Violent Behavior

Towards the end of the disease, many Alzheimer's patients become violent. We must remember that violence is a symptom of the disease, not the intention of the patient. Resistance, confrontation, and violence are actually ways of communicating. The patient is looking for something that we aren't providing.

Caregivers must focus their energy on finding ways of coping. There will be times, however, when confrontation can't be avoided. Where's our safety net? The film *"Dealing With Alzheimer's Disease: A Common Sense Approach To Communication,"* suggests the **FIVE-R** approach:

1. Remain calm

2. Respond to feelings

3. Reassure

4. Remove yourself

5. Return later

Forget jokes, arguments, or reasoning; it's time for action. You want to diffuse the situation as quickly as possible. Caregivers need to be clear and firm and to follow through. David Carroll, author of *When Your Loved One Has Alzheimer's*, believes caregivers should use "no" and "don't" when necessary.

We should also be direct. Rude as it sounds, the question, "What do you want?" may help to elicit a response from the patient. Yet violent behavior often puts patients and caregivers on a collision course. What can we do?

We can't change Alzheimer's disease. We can't change the patients. So we must change ourselves. Change starts with running interference and learning how to avoid caregiving obstacles. As the next chapter shows, running interference is a challenge.

CHAPTER 5

Running Interference

Topics

Misconceptions

Erratic Behavior

Wandering or Lost Patients

Staff Problems

Environment

Patient Anger

Well-Meant Advice

Targeting of the Elderly

Paperwork

The Happiness Myth

Rising Cost of Care

Caregiving is a lot like football. Some obstacles are expected, and others come as a complete surprise. What's the solution? We can run interference by identifying the obstacles and dealing with them before they deal with us.

Misconceptions about Alzheimer's are major obstacles for caregivers. Three common misconceptions: the diagnosis should always be divulged; explanations help patients; and relatives will get the disease. Let's take a closer look at each misconception.

Misconceptions:

Diagnosis Should Be Divulged

Should patients be told they have probable Alzheimer's? Margaret Drickamer, M.D., and Mark Lachs, M.D., M.P.H., discuss this question in the *New England Journal of Medicine*. They say patients in the early stages of the disease may understand the diagnosis and its implications.

"They may wish to make financial arrangements, settle personal affairs, or seek other medical advice," the authors note. But patients eventually lose the ability to make competent decisions. What's more, patients in the middle and final stages of the disease will forget the diagnosis.

Mom's doctor helped me to make the decision. I asked him if he was going to tell my mother she had probable Alzheimer's. "Would this help her?" he asked.

"No," I said. "It wouldn't change anything."

"Then I don't think we should tell her," he replied.

Disclosure also depends on the severity of the disease at the time of diagnosis. Each patient is different, and caregivers must do what they think is best. Of course, the patient's needs should come first.

"If you would just explain."

This misconception is based on otherwise sound patient education principles. But Alzheimer's patients aren't learning; they're unlearning, and we're not going to teach them anything. Day by day, cell by cell, relatives are watching a loved one die, and the emotional pain is unbearable.

Review may help patients in the early stage of the disease, but it does little for patients in the later stages. No matter how succinctly our review points are stated, the patient isn't going to remember them. I've had to come to terms with this reality.

Because of my experience as an educator, I believe in stating concepts, dividing them into subconcepts, reviewing periodically, and "learning by doing." None of these techniques work with my mother. However, my child-development training has been helpful.

Relatives Will Get Alzheimer's

They may not say it aloud, but every family caregiver fears he or she will get the disease. "I'm next!" a friend exclaimed.

Ronald C. Peterson, M.D., Ph.D., director of the Alzheimer's Project at the Mayo Clinic, shed some light on the statistics at Mayo's first conference on the disease.

A retrospective study by Mayo Clinic researchers indicates the disease was called dementia, senility, or old age in the past. "The disease itself isn't increasing," Dr. Peterson said, "but the absolute number of cases is increasing." This increase is due to the growing population of older people.

The human brain, an electrical and chemical organ, is a miracle of nature. Nobody really knows why brain cells die. According to Dr. Peterson, if you have a primary relative with the disease—mother, father, brother, sister—your risk of developing Alzheimer's is about 19 percent.

"We're becoming more aware of what constitutes Alzheimer's disease," he said. Mayo researchers are currently studying risk factors, biological markers, genetics, the role of amyloid (a protein deposited in the brain), and drug treatments. Hopefully this research will lead to identification of early predictors of the disease.

The book *Alzheimer's: A Caregiver's Guide and Sourcebook*, contains some encouraging news. Author Howard Gruetzner, M. Ed., says the risk factor for primary relatives "is no higher or only slightly higher than the risk factor for the general population." So family members may as well put their worry energy into enjoying life.

Erratic Behavior

Erratic behavior is a companion to Alzheimer's disease. Within minutes, the patient's behavior can change from passive to active, inquisitive to withdrawn, pleased to displeased. Words that worked yesterday may not work today.

Yesterday the patient liked chicken; today he or she hates it. Yesterday the patient liked to watch golf on television; today he or she hates it. Yesterday the patient enjoyed bathing; today he or she hates it. Caregivers can hardly keep pace with these erratic changes.

Disorientation contributes to erratic behavior as well. If a caregiver rearranges the family room furniture, the patient may lose all sense of direction and literally walk in circles. Traffic-pattern obstacles—wheelchairs, food trays, medical carts, and the like—are also confusing. The patient may mutter worriedly or ask, "Where is the door?"

Convincing Words and Body Language

Despite profound vocabulary loss, many patients have the ability to insert convincing words into conversation. A few big words and erect posture helped Mom convince the staff she was born in London, England. Actually it was my grandmother who was born in London and came to the U.S. when she was 16 years old. On another occasion, she almost had me convinced that the dry cleaner had ruined her coat.

"I want you to sue him!" she demanded.

I called the dry cleaner and talked with the supervisor. "Oh, I remember that coat," he said with some exasperation. "Your mother tried to wash it. She tossed the wet coat in a plastic trash bag and sent it out to be cleaned. We did our best, but the coat had already shrunk."

Intent on revenge, Mom wrote a nasty letter to the company. "You have no legal claim, Mom," I said. "Please don't mail the letter." She took my advice, and I have the letter in my files. Caregivers need to check out convincing stories and body language.

Plateau Periods

Alzheimer's can level off temporarily, and these respites are called plateau periods. F. Jacob Huff, writing in *Language, Memory, and Aging*, points out that plateau periods are not periods of remission. Researchers have made progress but, as of now, the disease is still irreversible.

Caregivers may be lulled by plateau periods and fall into a "things aren't as bad as I thought" mindset. When Mom has a plateau period, I tend to plan and expect too much. Once I took her to a Saturday afternoon movie, a romantic action drama with lots of special effects.

Mom didn't go to sleep, as I had anticipated, but stared at the screen intently. I mistook her attention for comprehension. After the movie, she said, "What was all that about? I didn't understand a thing. Did you?" Trying to follow the plot was so exhausting, Mom went right to bed.

Even though the patient is in a plateau period, it's best to keep things simple. Experts recommend setting up a routine and sticking to it. For example, Mom and I always have lunch at the same restaurant. The food is good and the surroundings are familiar. Mom can order what she likes because she knows the menu. We're both safe.

Wandering or Lost Patients

At least two out of three people with Alzheimer's and related disorders live at home, according to *Abnormal Psychology in a Changing World*. Eventually these patients need continuous care. While the caregiver is preparing food, doing the laundry, or even in the bathroom, patients may walk out the door. And most can't find their way back.

Residents of assisted-living facilities also get lost. Mom called me several times from the mall, asking me to come get her. "The bus left without me, and I can't find my way out of this damn place," she said. Getting lost is embarrassing for the patient and stressful for the caregiver.

When Mom fell and broke her shoulder, she couldn't remember where she lived. The doctor asked me to buy an identification bracelet for her as a precaution.

"Why do I need a identification bracelet?" Mom asked. "I know my own name."

"If you fall and hit your head, Mom, you could be knocked out," I said. "Then you wouldn't be able to speak."

The bracelet became a source of strife between us. Some days Mom wore it, some days she didn't. And she kept losing it. Ostuni and Santo Pietro, the authors of *Getting Through,* advise getting a Medic-Alert® bracelet inscribed with the words "memory disorder." This is an excellent suggestion, but one my mother would have opposed.

Despite security measures, some patients wander away from nursing homes. All of their remaining intelligence seems to focus on escape. After patients return to the nursing home, communication can be strained. Caregivers need to assure patients that they have their welfare at heart and are happy to see them.

Chapter eight, *"Do You Hear What I Hear?"* contains tips for jump-starting communication.

Staff Problems

New and temporary staff may be unfamiliar with the patient's case. Moreover, staff members can get so used to patients that they don't see the obvious.

Elizabeth was going to take her mother shopping. When she arrived at the nursing home, she found her mother was indecently dressed, wearing a jacket with a deep V that revealed her underwear, which was falling off. Elizabeth found a blouse (it didn't match the outfit) and redressed her mother.

The nursing supervisor was surprised to learn the state of the patient's undress. "Your mother is such a confident person, we probably didn't check her carefully," she said. "We'll be more careful in the future."

Poor Communication

Shift changes can be an obstacle for family caregivers. Every Sunday morning, Bill drove to the nursing home and picked his mother up for church. He had been doing this for months, but this wasn't communicated to the entire staff. Nurses would call and ask him if he was picking up his mother.

So Bill started calling the staff to remind them of the arrangement. That didn't work either, and Bill became exasperated. "They could leave a note at the desk or put it on the calendar," he said angrily. "That's not too complicated, is it?"

Contact a supervisor if you are dissatisfied with staff communication. End the exchange with an offer of help, such as, "Is there anything you would like me to do?" This lets management know you're a team player and not a complainer.

Meddling

Some families have been harmed by meddling staff members. One Florida family reserved a nursing home bed for their father. A visiting nurse who was opposed to nursing home placement gave the supervisor false information. She told the supervisor that family members had decided to let their father stay in his apartment. Fortunately, the supervisor had the good sense to check with the family caregiver.

"I'm confused," she began. "We had reserved a bed for your father, and I hear you've changed your mind? You don't want the bed?"

"Now I'm confused," the caregiver replied. "Of course we want the bed. Where did you get that idea?"

The caregiver and supervisor managed to piece the facts together. Most nursing homes have waiting lists, and this family nearly lost their father's place. But more importantly, the nurse's actions went against medical recommendations.

Family members contacted the patient's doctor, a geriatric specialist, social services, and the visiting nurse's employer. Although the nurse apologized to the family, the apology didn't negate her unprofessional behavior. Deciding to place a loved one in a nursing home is painful enough without the added pain of meddling.

Environment

Lady Bird Johnson once said, "I believe one of the great problems for us as individuals is the depression and tension resulting from existence in a world that is increasingly less pleasing to the eye."

Depressed surroundings lead to depressed thoughts. In turn, these thoughts lead to depressed conversation or, in some cases, no conversation. We forget that Alzheimer's patients, despite their mental impairments, still respond to beauty—fresh flowers, colorful pictures, china displayed in a hutch.

Patients respond even more when they're involved in decorating. Caregivers can involve patients in planning, such as choosing carpet and deciding where to put things. Being asked even simple yes and no questions makes patients feel valued. "Is this chair comfortable?" "Do you like this color?"

It is also important for patients to have personal possessions in their rooms. Mom has a well-loved and worn rocking chair, a maple chest of drawers, a bargello picture I made for her, and family photos. We also give her seasonal plants for the windowsill.

Notes and Notices

At the first Mayo Clinic Alzheimer's Disease Center conference, Bobbie Speich, L.P.N., N.H.A., said labels help patients find and store things. Drawers could be labeled "underwear," "socks," "gloves," etc. My mother's magazines are stored in a separate file box labeled with her name.

Seasonal or holiday decorations and an activities calendar help patients keep track of the days of the week. Speich advised posting the calendar in a common area, such as the dining room. The calendar also sends the message, "Things are happening here."

Mom became excited when she saw that nursery school children were coming on Halloween. The calendar listing and visit put a sparkle in her dialogue.

"Oh the children were adorable," she said later. "They came in their costumes. I told the little girl I had a treat for her. Those kids were so adorable."

Overcrowding

Overcrowding affects patients and the words they say. Tempers flair when too many people are crammed in a small space. As one nursing home resident explained, "This is a nice place, but it's too crowded. It makes people angry. Last week I saw two fistfights."

The patient who has just vacated a home or an apartment is bound to feel crowded. Maybe the nursing home isn't really crowded, it just looks crowded because of all the clutter. Experts advise cutting down on clutter for aesthetic and safety reasons.

Small measures, such as storing magazines in a lucite wall unit, can do a lot to solve the clutter problem. Family members can help by storing seasonal items at home. However, the patient will probably need to be reminded about this storage arrangement.

Patient Anger

Anger is a major obstacle for family and professional caregivers. Certainly, Alzheimer's patients have lots to be angry about: the diagnosis, being old and sick, living with adult children, and unresolved issues. Each topic is enough to trigger an emotional explosion.

Anger at the Diagnosis

It happens all the time. The patient senses things aren't going well, refuses to complete the psychometrics tests, and leaves the doctor's examining room.

Stunning as the diagnosis is, the patient may need time to get things in order.

Out of date wills may need to be revised and the patient may want to sign a living will. Possessions and property could be given to family members. Oral histories could be tape recorded for future generations. Photographs could be labeled and put in albums. Some patients write their biographies or compile grandparent books.

To outsiders these actions may look like frantic behavior, the last sputtering of a candle before it goes out. Not so. In truth, these actions return some control to the patient, helping him or her work through the stages of grief.

Some patients are comforted by the diagnosis, however, and it can help to ease self-worry. "Now I know what is wrong with me," one patient said. "That makes me feel better."

Anger at Living With Children

There aren't enough assisted-living facilities or nursing homes to accommodate the rising tide of patients, so caregivers are caring for them at home. According to recent Census Bureau figures, more than one million Americans age 65 or older live with their adult children.

Will this parent-child relationship work? Pat Shapiro, writing in the *AARP Bulletin*, thinks the partial success of the arrangement depends on the "art of communicating." In her article, "My House Is Your House,"

Shapiro says old relationships and unresolved feelings interfere with good communication.

To foster better communication Shapiro lists these tips:

• Discuss issues before the parent moves in.

• Plan schedules (bathroom, television, laundry, etc.).

• Set mutual boundaries and limits (special chair for patient, etc.).

• Discuss the unspeakable (living wills, death, funeral arrangements).

In addition, Shapiro says people need some space and privacy. This gives the patient a place to calm down, take a nap, and rethink things. Certainly, communication is better when participants are rested and amenable.

Anger at Being Old

Despite attractive surroundings, a competent staff, and a bevy of activities, many nursing home residents are angry. One caregiver commented to an administrator, "This is a beautiful facility, staffed by kind people, with good meals, and a wonderful activities program. Why is everyone so angry?"

"They're angry because they're old," replied the administrator. "And we can't change that."

When anger drives dialogue, sentences get shorter, voices get louder, and "loaded words" are used.

Learning to handle patient anger is a trial-and-error process. Three approaches helped me to diffuse my mother's anger and they may help you:

- "I love you, and I'm not going to argue with you."

- "I can understand why you're angry. I would be angry, too."

- "I'll get to that as soon as I can."

To be honest, I'm not sure why these approaches work. The word "love" in the first statement can stop anger quickly. "I know you love me," Mom replies. Perhaps the agreeing tone of the second approach validates her feelings. I think the last approach works because I always keep my promises.

Anger at Unresolved Issues

All caregivers bring unresolved issues to the task. Psychotherapist Harriet Goldhor Lerner, Ph.D., writes about these issues in her book, *The Dance of Anger*. "Remember that we all contain within us—and act out with others—family patterns and unresolved issues that are passed down from many generations," she writes.

Short-term memories are eroded by Alzheimer's disease, but long-term memories may be as clear as if they happened yesterday. The spouse of an alcoholic may have bittersweet memories. I know this from experience because my mother often talks about my father's alcoholism.

Some days Mom can't say enough good things about Dad. "Your father bought me anything I wanted. I wanted a fur coat, and the next day we went shopping for one." Mom often gets out the jewelry Dad gave her and shares her memories with me.

Other days Mom is bitter. "I know you're not supposed to speak ill of the dead, but damn your father to hell!" she exclaimed. "I wasted all those years."

Clearly Mom is dealing with polarized feelings—fiercely negative and fiercely positive—and trying to resolve them. Years ago she wouldn't have discussed Dad's alcoholism with anyone. Now she discusses it openly.

Much as we would like to, caregivers can't erase the pain of the past. On the one hand, we're glad the patient is sharing these memories with us. On the other hand, talking about these long-term memories upsets the patient.

The siblings of caregivers may have unresolved issues as well, such as being the baby of the family.

"My younger sister couldn't accept the fact that Mom had Alzheimer's," explained one caregiver. "She was in complete denial, still the baby, and this made decision making harder."

The anger of unresolved issues is a challenge for caregivers. Dr. Lerner suggests two responses: sharing something personal and dialogue. I've tried both techniques, and they both work. When Mom tells stories about Dad's alcoholism, I listen and assure her that I remember the incidents. Assurance flows naturally into dialogue—usually brief, but we're talking.

Well-Meant Advice

Nothing disturbs caregivers quite as much as well-meant advice. The advice may come from relatives who seldom visit or strangers who are totally unfamiliar with the case. Well-meant advice doesn't help the caregivers who are on the "front lines."

Dealing with the advice can sap the caregiver's energy. A staff person asked me, "Do you really think your mother needs to go into nursing care? She seems to be doing so well." For months I had agonized over the decision and her comment not only hurt me, it haunted me.

Well-meant advice often includes "you should" statements that ignite the caregiver's anger as quickly as a match to tinder. Well-meant advice is usually based on generalities, not the details of day-to-day caregiving. Why don't people think before they speak?

Leo Buscaglia, Ph.D., author of *Loving Each Other*, thinks we have to monitor our language. "It is essential to know, if we desire to communicate, that we must be careful about the words we use, for they may be using us!" he writes.

Well-meant advice is an emotional obstacle for caregivers who replay the words over and over in their minds. About all we can do is thank people for their advice, pick and choose what is helpful, and ignore the rest. We have other things to do.

Targeting of the Elderly

Alzheimer's patients are prime targets for scams, "bait and switch" schemes, overpricing, and outright fraud. The first month Mom lived in Minnesota, she received enough scam mail to fill two giant-sized garbage cans. Mom was living with us at the time, and the more letters I read the angrier I became.

A number of letters arrived in official-looking envelopes marked "Open Immediately," "Reply Within 5 Days," "Personal," "Urgent," and "To be opened by addressee only." The letters asked for money and promised benefits too good to be true.

An envelope with a Chicago postmark contained a bill for auto parts. Mom hadn't bought any auto parts and didn't have a license or a car. I wrote the Minnesota attorney general's office and included a packet of sample scams with my letter. Several days later, I received a call from a lawyer in St. Paul.

"Thanks for contacting us," she said. "We see the same scams in different states." She gave me a phone number to call to stop the junk mail and said the attorney general's office was investigating one business I had reported.

What does targeting the elderly have to do with communication? Well, vulnerable adults like my mother believe the scams. The scams cause financial losses and lead to arguments. Mom and I had a running battle about the letters and the prizes that came—kitchen magnets, egg separators, keychains, and other junk.

Sadder still, Mom had been spending an alarming amount of money on international lotteries. Lottery forms arrived from England, Ireland, and Canada. Mom wanted to enter lotteries to make up for the money she had squandered. When I objected to this, she exclaimed, "It's my money, and I can spend it any way I want to!"

The targeting of the vulnerable and elderly is epidemic, an international disgrace, a sad commentary on today's ethics. I urge all caregivers to take action against these scams. Alzheimer's patients may not be able to defend themselves, but we can defend them.

Paperwork

Caregivers are inundated by paperwork: insurance forms, investment reports, letters, bank statements, and tax records. I have become Mom's personal secretary, and the paperwork blizzard is getting worse. We bought two cabinets to hold all of her files.

Paperwork alters communication if for no other reason than it takes time away from the patient. Often the patient has lost important documents—birth certificates, deeds, wills, titles. Losing the documents is humiliating, and patients get defensive.

And many Alzheimer's patients have left a paperwork trail behind them. Attempts to follow this trail cause discord among family caregivers and patients. While the caregiver is working feverishly, the patient may be thinking, "What have you done for me lately?" Chances are the caregiver is ignoring his or her own paperwork to help the patient.

Finances are all mixed up in Mom's mind, and she covers her confusion with anger. One day she was especially critical. I didn't want to argue with my mother, so I said, "I'm doing the best I can."

"You may be doing your best," she responded, "but it isn't good enough." I decided to react with silence. Caregivers don't have to fill in every blank in conversation.

The Happiness Myth

As society scrambles to keep pace with the increasing number of Alzheimer's cases, new support services and jobs are being created. A number of these workers have no geriatric training and haven't been around elderly people very much.

For example, a young activities director was asked to describe her program. "We let them [Alzheimer's patients] do what they want, and we make them happy," the director said. She isn't the only person who believes if we have enough activities and services for patients, they will be happy. It's true that patients in the early stage of Alzheimer's may benefit from these things, but patients in the final stage don't.

What makes people happy? Good health, friends, learning, hobbies, and travel all contribute to happiness. The Alzheimer's patient's health is failing, friends are dying, new information isn't retained, hobbies are forgotten, and travel is rarely an option.

What's more, many patients are grieving—mourning the loss of vision, hearing, walking ability, bladder control, sexual performance, and other physical failings. Caregivers can't make patients happy; we can only make them comfortable and keep them safe.

Rising Cost of Care

Insurance reimbursements often fall short of actual costs. Families pay for the indirect costs of caregiving, too—food, notions, postage, transportation, and more. The result? The family budget is stretched to the maximum or falls short.

"I'm afraid we'll be broke," a worried caregiver told me.

This fear is well-founded. An Associated Press article, published in the *Physicians Financial News* in October 1994, says it costs $213,000 a year to care for one patient. In the article, Edward Truschke, president of the Alzheimer's Association, is quoted as saying, "The disease is draining the resources of this country and its citizens at a greater rate than we thought."

Nobody can accurately predict how long an Alzheimer's patient will live. The patient could be in a nursing home for 8 to 10 years, and costs are rising. Many families are burdened with costs until—and long after—the patient's death.

All of the forces and obstacles discussed in this chapter join together to bombard speech. Alzheimer's patients are trying to find the words to express themselves. Caregivers are searching for the words to respond. The need to run interference only works to muddle communications further. Eliminating the interference wherever possible will leave you more time and energy for the important and challenging task of overcoming personal communication blockers—the subject of the next chapter.

CHAPTER 6

Personal Communication Blockers

Topics

Our Fears

Family Responsibilities

Caregiver's Anger

Guilt and More Guilt

Stress

Health Problems

Shame

Isolation

Parenting Our Parents

Anticipatory Grief

Our Fears

Communication is shaped by the personal issues, conscious and unconscious, that caregivers bring to the process. Fear is one issue. Caregivers have many fears, including fear for their own safety.

Fear of Injury

As Alzheimer's progresses, the patients become uncooperative and refuse to do things, like take a bath or change into clean clothes. These refusals are called catastrophic reactions. Refusals aren't stubbornness, they're mental catastrophes for patients, who have forgotten skills and objects.

My mother doesn't know how to comb her hair anymore. The nurses wanted to fix her hair and help her change into a dress for Thanksgiving, but Mom wouldn't let them do it. She has had other catastrophic reactions as well.

When I arrived at nursing care one day, Mom refused to wear a coat over her blazer. "It's really cold, Mom," I explained. "Better wear both."

"No. It won't work."

"What won't work?" I asked.

"The coat won't go over it," Mom said.

"If you hold the cuffs of the blazer, I think your coat will go on," I suggested.

"No, it won't work," she insisted, tossing the blazer on a chair. "I'm not wearing it." She fumbled with her coat and began to put it on. She didn't seem to know what to do with the buttons, so I buttoned it for her.

The coat incident is mild compared with the violence some caregivers encounter. A kind and helpful woman in the past, one patient began punching her husband in the stomach. Another nursing home resident hit someone with his crutches. I wondered if my mother's anger would ever become physical.

Three days after I had laser surgery for a detaching retina, I took Mom out for our usual midweek lunch. She was in a bad mood, became angry, and started thrashing her arms about. Would she hit me? I moved as close to the car door as possible.

Changing the subject calmed her. I haven't forgotten the incident, though, and the awful feeling of being afraid. For despite her medical problems, Mom is a sturdy woman, taller than I, with a larger bone structure and surprising strength.

Fear of Being Next

Every family caregiver I have talked with—and I've talked with many during the last 12 years—has expressed the fear of being next. This fear is magnified by the knowledge that we can't do anything about it. Writer Judith Viorst describes this fear eloquently in her book, *Necessary Losses*.

Viorst believes that our parents' aches and pains remind us of our own mortality. "We recognize that we're soon to lose our shield between us and death, and that after they are gone, it will be our turn," she says.

With each passing year, I look more like my mother. And this, more than anything, reminds me that I'm next. As my facial muscles sag, my cookie-dough features are melting to match Mom's. Like other caregivers, I feel a sense of mourning for my mother and myself. But I think there's more to the "I'm next" fear.

Because Alzheimer's is a disease of the elderly, most family caregivers are middle-aged. Just when we thought we were grown-up and independent, parents are yanked back into our lives. We have to work to avoid falling back into old childhood patterns. "Everything seems up for grabs," summarizes Viorst.

Fear of the Elderly

Unlike other cultures, our society tends to separate the elderly from the young. This lack of contact contributes to a fear of the elderly and ill. Too many people think nursing homes are places to avoid. "We don't get many visitors," a nurse explained. "They don't visit because they don't want to think about getting old."

The less we know about Alzheimer's patients, the less we empathize with them. Our lack of empathy comes through in verbal communication and body language. Gerald Goodman, Ph.D., and Glenn Esterly, authors of *The Talk Book,* believe many elderly people suffer from "empathy starvation."

As relatives and friends die, the remaining elderly lose opportunities for sharing. Alzheimer's patients find themselves discussing topics that younger listeners don't understand—songs, styles, slang, memories. So the patient tries to explain things, which puts a strain on language skills.

"Now it takes a lot of effort to say little," the authors note.

One by one Mom's friends are moving into nursing care. They rarely speak to one another, however, because they have similar mental impairments. What can caregivers do? According to Goodman and Esterly, there are two solutions to "empathy starvation."

- Approach the elderly person (in this case, the Alzheimer's patient) as an amateur historical researcher. Instead of asking yes or no questions, I ask prompting questions. "I remember getting lost at the fair. Can you tell me about that?"

- Compare parallel experiences. For example, the caregiver and patient may like old-time movie musicals. Mom likes to discuss cooking, probably because she doesn't do it any more.

There's a third solution, I believe, and that's sharing memories about family mementos. When Mom was a young woman, she was a secretary and a stocking model. I have a pair of her gray silk stockings at home, the kind with embroidered "clocks" on them. Seeing the stockings and other family mementos usually gets Mom talking.

Family Responsibilities

When we love someone, we gladly do things for them and with them. However, the caregiver who has spent most of the day helping an Alzheimer's patient has little energy left. This is particularly true of women.

A U.S. House of Representatives' document reports the "average woman" in our country will spend 17 years raising her children and another 18 years taking care of aging parents. But more men are becoming caregivers these days. Like female caregivers, the men find themselves torn in opposite directions.

Responsibility to Partner

There are never enough hours in a day. We have little time for our partners and less time for ourselves. For a variety of reasons, caregivers may be reluctant to ask for help.

Like any chronic illness, Alzheimer's can bring families closer together or drive them apart. My husband and I keep communication lines open by turning off the television at mealtime, accepting few evening invitations, and sharing our feelings. One of the most loving gifts John gives me is the gift of listening.

With my husband's help, I'm able to keep caregiving in perspective. And this helps me to help my mother. I never know what's going through Mom's mind, and one day she blurted, "You married a fine man."

"Yes, I did," I replied.

"And you still love him," Mom continued.

"I love him more every day," I said. Mom nodded her head in agreement and lapsed into thought. Then she turned, made eye contact with me, and said quietly, "I loved your father, too."

Responsibility to Children

After taking care of the patient, the caregiver may rush home, gulp supper, and race off to the high school play. Nobody can keep up this pace for long. Tired caregivers aren't good communicators, that's for sure, and our blunt language yields blunt replies.

People keep telling me I'm a member of the sandwich generation, but that doesn't change anything. I continue to parent adult daughters, grandparent the twins, and care for my mother. My "sandwich" has become a club sandwich.

Children may not understand Alzheimer's disease, so we'll have to tell them. Picture books can help younger children, and the Alzheimer's Association has published a helpful pamphlet, "Alzheimer's disease: Especially for Teenagers."

At Thanksgiving, I updated our younger daughter on Mom's condition. "She may not recognize you or talk much," I said. Mom did recognize our daughter, said hello, and then was silent throughout dinner. But she enjoyed her food and being with the family, especially when we all joined hands.

Responsibility to Other Relatives

A number of caregivers are also caring for other relatives. The caregiver's spouse may have cancer, for example, or the caregiver may have teenagers in trouble. Making "small talk" is a challenge when all we want to do is cry.

Mom's younger sister, her only remaining sibling, lives in New Jersey. Although Mom knows her sister has health problems, she can't remember them. "She's in a bad way," Mom says.

Much as I would like to, I can't rescind the ravages of time and disease. To keep communication lines open, I talk with my aunt on the phone and write her notes. I also keep my brother and his wife informed about Mom's health.

Career Demands

To meet the rising costs of care, family caregivers must continue to work and be productive. There may be early morning meetings to attend and continuing education units to earn. Some caregivers must learn entirely new skills.

Caregiver stress soars when work responsibilities are coupled with caregiving responsibilities. To further complicate things, middle-aged caregivers may be offered career opportunities too good to pass up.

Can career advancements blend with caregiving? The answer is yes, but the caregiver will probably have to give up something—personal reading, day trips, evening concerts, hobbies, contact with friends, sleep, and the like. The caregiver may believe that life is passing him or her by, and this can lead to anger.

Caregiver's Anger

If you observe caregivers over time, you realize many are angry. Their anger is revealed in impatience, terse sentences, and blunt body language. I think a lot of the anger caregivers feel comes from loss of time.

Anger at Loss of Time

When caregivers lose control of their time, they also lose control of their lives. In her book, *Stress and the Healthy Family,* Dolores Curran examines the role that time plays in family stress. "Some families live with stress at a peak level constantly," Curran observes. Some danger signs she cites:

• No time for relaxation.

• Feeling that time is passing too quickly.

• Talk about when life was simpler.

• Lack of "me time" or "couple time."

• Guilt at not being able to do everything for everyone.

The caregivers who have an Alzheimer's patient living at home feel all of these stressors. "Don't start in, Ma," one caregiver said angrily. "Just don't start in." Of course his mother took the comment as a challenge, raised the ante, and her complaints became louder.

Being the only caregiver can keep the embers of anger glowing. However, there are solutions to time-based anger. We can discuss our angry feelings with a trusted partner or friend, exercise regularly, and find a quiet place to be alone.

Anger at Being the Only Caregiver

These days family members are often scattered throughout the country or even the world. In many cases, it's the family member who lives closest to the patient who becomes the caregiver. These caregivers have little or no time to rest or regroup.

"Nobody else helps, and I'm tired of being responsible," admitted one caregiver.

Fatigue can lead to anger and a feeling of "Why is this happening to me?" But the news isn't all bad. Anger counteracts stress, according to Matthew McKay, Ph.D, Peter Robers, Ph.D., and Judith McKay, R.N., authors of *When Anger Hurts*. In fact, the authors say the sole function of anger is to stop stress.

How does this work? Well, anger blocks off our painful emotions. In addition, it helps relieve the physical symptoms of stress, such as muscle tension. And the authors say, "Anger can discharge stress that develops when you are frustrated in the search for something you need or want." Finally, anger can motivate and push us towards positive actions.

Being the only caregiver causes communication undercurrents. The caregiver's voice may sound tired or resentful. No matter how we feel, caregivers need to speak in warm, empathetic tones and not rush patients.

Guilt and More Guilt

Many caregivers—usually women—feel guilty for not doing a better job. I feel guilty for lots of things: not having more time, getting behind on Mom's filing, and feeling estranged from her. A lot of my guilt stems from caregiving and career conflicts.

My guilty thoughts usually begin with the words "I should." Some examples:

- "I should have moved Mom sooner."

- "I should live closer to Mom."

- "I should give up writing and devote more time to Mom."

- "I should not involve John in caregiving; this is my mother, not his."

- "I should be a better caregiver."

- "I should do more for the other nursing care residents."

Guilt is a nonproductive emotion, and I work hard to combat it. David Burns, M.D., examines the roots of guilt in his best-selling book, *Feeling Good*. He says guilt can be replaced with enlightened behavior, namely empathy.

To determine whether guilt is healthy or self-defeating, Dr. Burns asks readers to answer four questions:

1. Did you consciously do something "bad?" For example, did you say you were going to buy groceries and not follow through?

2. Are you labeling yourself a "bad" person because of your actions? Some days I convince myself I'm a poor caregiver when I'm really a competent caregiver. I am fortunate to have a supportive husband who helps me keep my caregiving in balance.

3. Are you feeling regretful or remorseful? Certainly, there are days when all caregivers feel this way, if for no other reason than they didn't get as much accomplished as they wanted to.

4. Are you learning from your mistakes and changing your behavior? I've learned a lot from Mom, and this book represents the changes I've made in communicating with her.

The bottom line is that guilt scrambles communication. Surely the caregivers who learn to empathize with patients can learn to empathize with themselves. Finding the words is easier when a generous dash of empathy is added to conversation.

Stress

A recent medical advisor column, syndicated nationally by the Palo Alto Medical Foundation, reported that stress can lead to poorer immune systems, more infectious illnesses, and depression in caregivers. The article cites a study by Leonard Pearlin, a researcher at the University of California in San Francisco.

Pearlin's research indicates that caregivers develop "secondary stress." Contributing factors to secondary stress include family conflicts, financial problems, fewer social or leisure activities, work responsibilities, self-doubt, and feeling locked in an unwanted role. The caregiver who feels locked in an unwanted role isn't going to be a good communicator, that's for sure.

Communicating with patients may become a stressful experience. *Alzheimer's: A Caregiver's Guide and Sourcebook* contains a 20-point worksheet for measuring staff stress from dementia care. Four of the points pertain to speech:

- The staff person is tired of the patient repeating things.

- The patient's babbling and rambling speech gets on the staff person's nerves.

- Communicating with dementia patients is hard for the staff person.

- The staff person has trouble talking with the patient's family.

Caregivers may find it helpful to make a list of personal stressors. For example, three of my top stressors are money worries, writing deadlines, and holiday preparations. I can tell that Mom picks up on my stress.

A couple of times the stress of caregiving has prompted migraine headaches. I've been taking estrogen for nearly 12 years. Migraine headaches are a side effect of estrogen, and every three months or so I have one. Fortunately, I only have auras, dazzling displays of lines, shapes, and colors—not full-blown headaches. Still, the auras are debilitating and I have to lie down until they pass. Scary as they are, the auras force me to slow down and take care of myself.

Health Problems

Caregiver stress can lead to a variety of health problems. According to the Alzheimer's Association, some examples of stress-related illnesses are:

- colds/flu

- insomnia

- headaches

- poor appetite

- overeating

- constipation or diarrhea

- heart palpitations

- high blood pressure

- indigestion

- cold hands and feet

- asthma

Neglecting our health doesn't do anything for the patient. If we're sick, we're not very good caregivers and we run the risk of infecting patients. Keep in mind that the patient may not share concerns for the caregiver's health.

For example, Mom called and asked me to take her to lunch. I apologized and said I was going to have my eyes checked.

"Why do you need to have your eyes checked?" she asked.

"The doctor is going to check my laser surgery," I said.

"What surgery?"

"Remember, I told you I had surgery on my eye?"

"Oh," Mom said. "Well, I want to go to lunch."

"I can't take you to lunch today," I replied, trying to speak in a soothing voice.

"O.K." Mom said angrily.

The tone of Mom's voice told me my refusal was far from being O.K. I knew I had hurt her but there was nothing I could do about it. Then too, I've noticed Mom likes to talk about her ailments and nobody else's.

Shame

Family members may be ashamed that someone from their "genetic pool" has probable Alzheimer's disease. Where does this shame come from? In *Understanding*

Shame, Eunice Cavanaugh, M.Ed., M.S.W., gives insights into the origins of shame. According to Cavanaugh, three contributing factors are undesirable life change, aging and illness, and family loyalty.

She points out that people who feel shame may not realize it. "All we know is that we're uncomfortable," she writes.

Cavanaugh believes that seeing aging and illness threatens our own autonomy. So we're back to the "I'm next" response. The family balance may depend on everyone staying the same—but the patient isn't the same. Worse, the patient may be declining at a rapid rate.

According to Cavanaugh, shame may be denial in disguise. Family members may unconsciously believe that denying the diagnosis will somehow make Alzheimer's disease go away. "We can be pulled into the shame-anxiety cycle regardless of how accomplished or productive we have been in the past," she writes.

The truth is that going public with the diagnosis helps others. Former President Reagan's disclosure of probable Alzheimer's disease did a lot to counter ignorance and shame. His courageous disclosure raised public awareness of the disease and its symptoms around the world.

Isolation

Just when they need it most, caregivers have little or no time to socialize. Despite the best of intentions, the caregiver may become isolated. Nancy Gnaedinger explains isolation in her article, "The Alzheimer's Household: Who Cares for the Caregivers?"

Gnaedinger says the demands of caregiving and the time involved can reduce the caregiver's social life to a few hours a week. Slowly but surely, the caregiver's circle of friends shrinks. What's more, isolation narrows communication and leads to depression.

Caregivers can ease their burdens by plugging into community support systems and getting on with their lives. I know writing is a solitary occupation, so I balance it with family activities, committee work, and club memberships.

Parenting Our Parents

Many articles and books describe caring for an Alzheimer's patient as role reversal. This notion is false. No matter how much caregiving I do, my mother will never be my child. However, I can take over some parenting duties and make sure Mom gets good medical care. But even this is painful.

Mom's mini-strokes and probable Alzheimer's disease damaged the "number center" in her brain. She became an addictive spender and bought whatever caught her fancy. When I put her on a restricted budget, she reopened an account I had closed and solicited money from friends.

No matter what I said or did, she wouldn't stop spending money. Another resident had a bright red coat and

Mom decided she needed one. "Please don't buy a coat," I implored. "You have four winter coats already."

"But I don't have a red one," she said angrily.

"We have to conserve your funds, Mom. Don't buy the coat."

The next day Mom bought the coat and paid for it with a "kited" check. She had written three other checks with insufficient funds, and the bank was getting worried. So was I. I confiscated her charge cards and took over management of her funds.

"I'm your mother, and you're my daughter," she screamed. "It's my money, and I want it now!"

Becoming Mom's caregiver made me the primary target of her anger. But caregivers can take steps to counter anger. In *When Anger Hurts,* McKay and colleagues list six steps that can help. I've condensed the steps and added personal comments.

1. *Find ways to reinforce others.* In other words, stick to your principles and praise the patient. When Mom gets upset, I reinforce her with one-sentence replies. "You did a good job, Mom." "You're a kind person."

2. *Take care of your own needs.* Sometimes Mom makes plans for my time without consulting me, such as planning an afternoon of shopping. My reply: "I don't have time to do that today." Or I volunteer to purchase items for her.

3. *Develop a support and nourishment system.* My support system is my husband, family members, and

other caregivers. Each caregiver has his or her own idea of nourishment, and one of mine is curling up with a good book.

4. *Set clear limits.* This step to responsibility was easy for me because of my early childhood education training. I have learned to accept Mom's behavior and adjust to it.

5. *Learn to negotiate assertively.* This step is hard for me because I believe in tactful language and lead-in sentences. Mom understands neither. So I use blunt questions such as, "What do you want?"

6. *Let go.* The authors of *When Anger Hurts* say letting go also involves casting off solutions and relationships that are unrewarding. Caregivers may cast off coping strategies that don't work. Letting go also means accepting the finality of Alzheimer's disease.

Anticipatory Grief

Abnormal Psychology in a Changing World describes Alzheimer's disease as a funeral that never ends. Living with someone who has Alzheimer's may seem like living with a stranger, these writers say, "so profound are the changes in the person's personality and behavior." I think this is the beginning of anticipatory grief.

The worst part about my anticipatory grief is seeing my mother's interests and talents fade away. She used to be a fantastic gardener, for example, and landscaped the Long Island house with a colorful profusion of flowers, shrubs, and trees. Her garden was a celebration of life. Today she thinks the artificial violet on the windowsill is real and can't identify common house plants.

In the book *The Anatomy of Bereavement*, Beverly Raphael points out that anticipatory grief affects the dying person and those close to him or her. "The first responses to news or awareness of a fatal condition are usually those of shock, numbness, disbelief, and denial," Raphael says.

With anticipatory grief, caregivers may bounce from one level of mourning to another. One day we're in denial and the next day we're back to shock. Raphael says these feelings give way to questions like "Why me?" "Why my mother or father?"

My anticipatory grief got worse when I realized some retirement community residents were referring to Mom in the past tense. Dismantling her household and inquiring about funeral arrangements added to my grief.

It's hard to converse with the person we're mourning. Like other caregivers, I have times when I'm laughing on the outside and crying on the inside. I'm grieving for a marvelous mother and the roles she played in my life. To start with, I grieve for the helper who taught me to be kind to people.

I grieve for the gardener who grew lilies of the valley and tulips.

I grieve for the humorist who excelled at one-liners.

I grieve for the avid reader who read books by the dozen.

I grieve for the cook who baked orange sponge cakes.

I grieve for the crafter who knit sweaters and did needlepoint.

I grieve for the leader who was secretary and treasurer of the church women's group.

I grieve for the nurturer who helped me to believe in myself.

And when my mother is gone, I will grieve even more. But caregivers can't give up yet. We can foster communication and make the most of the days that remain. The next chapter is packed with tips on getting your message across.

CHAPTER 7

Getting Your Message Across

Topics

Personal Style

Voice

Eye Contact

Sharing Laughter

Reciprocal Body Language

Setting

Filling in the Blanks

Values of Silence

Reinforcement

Questions

Coping With Anger

Written and Visual Communication

This chapter contains tested tips for getting your message across. Whether or not the tips work will depend on the severity of the disease. Patients who have a flat affect (apathetic behavior) or are in a vegetative state aren't exactly equipped to get messages.

Still, there's a chance that a gentle touch and caring assurances will be heard. The title of a 1970 book by Elizabeth Kübler-Ross, M.D., applies here: *To Live Until We Say Good-bye.* Caregivers are communicating until they say good-bye to patients.

Personal Style

The caregiver's personal style can "make" or "break" communication. Ostuni and Santo Pietro, the authors of *Getting Through* say caregivers should evaluate their personal style. An evaluation questionnaire in their book includes such topics as voice, diction, vocabulary, hearing, humor, body language, and listening.

The questionnaire ends with a caution about placing value judgments on personal style. Readers are asked to answer the questions and check their answers later to become aware of their "inner gifts and resources."

Certainly each caregiver has unique talents to bring to the task. In fact, speaking style is part of the caregiver's identity. What's my style? More like sisters than mother and daughter, Mom and I talked in a fast, free-flowing style packed with one liners. Being quick on the repartee was almost a point of family pride at our house.

Maybe this was a sign of the times. Like most of our neighbors, we didn't have a television set, and conversation was a form of entertainment. On summer evenings, we sat on the front porch and talked. Neighbors sat on their front porches, too, and we could hear their voices in the darkness. Children played kick the can or chased fireflies while their parents talked, and the conversation lasted for hours.

No more. Mom can only follow short sentences and often misses the point of those. Differences in style are analogous to sending a message to a fax machine that isn't turned on. So I have shortened my style to match my mother's style.

One-Step Commands

Experts recommend using one-step commands with Alzheimer's patients, such as:

- "Use your walker."

- "Hold onto the safety bar."

- "Lie down now."

- "Turn up the volume on your hearing aid."

- "Put your arm in the sleeve."

- "Step down."

To soften the one-step commands, caregivers need to speak in gentle, feeling tones. We also need to be aware of regional accents and vocabulary. The patient from Massachusetts may not understand a caregiver from Louisiana and vice versa.

My mother doesn't understand the word "pop," common in Minnesota, but she knows what I mean if I say "soda." Minnesotans say "hot dish" and New Yorkers say "casserole." There are many other differences in language, and I try to talk "New York" to Mom.

Verbal Signals

Including verbal signals in conversation can help Alzheimer's patients get their bearings. I made an oral surgery appointment for my mother. As we got in the car I said, "I'm taking you to see the dentist today. This isn't your regular dentist, he's a Mayo Clinic dentist."

Because Alzheimer's patients lose their sense of direction, caregivers need to include directional signals in conversation as well. "We're going to turn left here and take the elevator." "The exit is at the end of this hallway." "We parked on the second level of the ramp."

Clinical psychologists Doreen Kotik-Harper and Robert G. Harper describe an unusual communications method in *Caring for the Alzheimer's Patient.* The method, which is called "backward chaining," has helped some patients, according to the authors.

Usually, directions are given in a forward progression, the authors point out, but "backward chaining" is just the opposite.

The Alzheimer's patient is escorted to the destination several times and "then familiarized with prominent locations increasingly distant from the destination," they explain. Only after the patient is familiar with the destination is he or she told about landmarks along the way.

Caregivers also need to prepare patients for curbs, stairs, and other changes in elevation. Signals reassure patients and let them know what to expect. Because the patient's memory is short, the caregiver may have to repeat these verbal signals several times.

The Editorial We

The more I interact with Alzheimer's patients, the more convinced I am that the editorial *we* should be dropped. Sentences like, "We are going to take a bath now" sound patronizing and demeaning. More importantly, the sentences are false. It isn't the caregiver who is going to take a bath, but the patient. "I'm going to help you take a bath," is more accurate language.

Of course there are times when the editorial we is appropriate. "We're going to the store now," for example. But in general, dropping the editorial we is clearer language and a sign of respect. (I have used the editorial we in this book because we share the common experience of caregiving.)

Voice

We've all met people whose voices annoy us. These voices may be whiny, squeaky, raspy, breathy, piercing, or worse. An unpleasant voice diverts attention away from the speaker's message. How do you sound to others? You may think you sound calm, but the patient may detect annoyance in your voice.

The patient is more apt to hear a message stated in an even voice and low pitch. If you don't know how your voice sounds, tape record a brief message. Listen to the tape with a trusted friend and determine the changes that need to be made.

Practice the changes and remember to speak slowly. Rapid speech sends the patient the message "I'm too busy to talk to you." This is an unwelcome, not to mention painful, message.

Framing

Communications expert Deborah Tannen, Ph.D., says voice helps to "frame" conversations. Dr. Tannen defines a frame as an indirect way of showing the meaning of words through voice. Is the speaker serious or kidding? Is the speaker sincere or insincere? Is the speaker rested or tired?

The listener determines the frame of the conversation by following voice clues—pitch, tone, and quality. This unconscious process is totally opposite of written communication, which relies on conscious clues such as "in closing."

Conversational frames are always nameless, according to Dr. Tannen. Trying to give the frame a name instantly alters communication. Speakers and listeners usually agree on conversational frames, Tannen says, and when they don't agree their conversation is reframed.

Not Answering

Not answering the patient can bring communication to a halt. When you don't answer a patient, you're sending him or her negative messages. Like rapid speech, message one is that the caregiver is rushed and busy. Message two is that the caregiver is preoccupied. Message three is that the caregiver doesn't care—and this may be the most harmful message of all.

Sarah was excited about going shopping for new slacks with her daughter. While her daughter drummed her fingers impatiently on a counter top, Sarah looked through racks of clothing. "Do you like these slacks?" she asked. No reply.

"Do you like these?" Sarah asked again. Her daughter looked at the slacks with such disdain that Sarah's enthusiasm vanished. "I guess I don't want any slacks," she said. Mother and daughter left the store in silence.

Although her daughter said nothing, Sarah heard hear message loud and clear: "I don't want to help you. I wish I was somewhere else." Every Alzheimer's patient deserves the courtesy of an answer, even if the answer is no.

Pitch

Pitch plays a leading role in how messages are transmitted. Changing the pitch of a word can alter its meaning completely. For example, the word "great" may sound like a superlative or a sarcastic comment. Dr. Tannen diagrams pitch in her book, *That's Not What I Meant!*

Lower pitch, considered by Dr. Tannen to be a sign of sincerity, is diagrammed with a lower line. Let's diagram the sentence, "That color really looks good on you."

That color

really looks

good on you.

However, if the caregiver raises his or her voice at the end of the sentence it would sound like false praise or sarcasm. The result? Alzheimer's patients, who are unsure about what's going on, become more unsure.

However, there are times when raising the pitch at the end of a sentence works. The caregiver may say, "I'll see you at the party tomorrow," raising the pitch to indicate anticipation. This works, especially if the sentence is combined with a smile.

It's best to avoid ending sentences on a higher pitch. While this has become a trend, ending sentences on a higher pitch turns every sentence into a question. Alzheimer's patients have enough questions in their lives without adding any more. Moreover, as Dr. Tannen points out, a higher pitch can come across as uncertainty or need for approval.

Pitch can also be insulting. Said in a certain way the sentence, "You really want to sit in this chair?" conveys disapproval or ridicule. In contrast, sentences totally devoid of inflection may sound angry to patients.

One caregiver walked into a patient's room, slammed a tray on the table, and said loudly, "Eat your supper."

Diagramming this sentence isn't necessary; it would be one horizontal line.

How did the patient respond? The patient used the only form of protest at his disposal and rejected the food. Needless to say, this didn't help the patient's health.

Eye Contact

Health professionals recommend making eye contact with Alzheimer's patients. While this is a valid recommendation, it's one I've found difficult to carry out. Mom is either looking the other way, distracted by events, or looking down at her lap.

The eyes have been called the windows of the soul. My mother's eyes are shuttered now, and making eye contact with her is painful. Yet Mom works at making eye contact with the twins. I guess the elderly are often attracted to the young.

Caregivers increase their chances of getting messages across if their eyes are level with the patient's eyes. Looking up at someone is uncomfortable and puts patients at a psychological disadvantage. On the other hand, sitting beside the patient or kneeling in front of him or her is encouraging body language.

Sharing Laughter

When I was growing up, Mom was so funny she could have been a stand-up comic. Once, Mom and her sister went into New York City to shop. Bloomingdale's was having a wig sale—obviously deals too good to pass up, because Mom bought a purple wig and her sister bought a pink one.

The Clifton girls, as they called themselves, put the wigs on and "strutted their stuff" all over town. Even complacent New Yorkers did a double take. After that shopping trip, just saying the word "wig" would send Mom into gales of laughter.

Now Mom's laughter is an exception, not the rule—an event that takes me by surprise. There are times, however, when something clicks in Mom's mind and she is almost herself. Although she is Protestant she occasionally attends mass.

"I went to mass this morning," Mom told me.

"That's nice," I replied.

"Oh, I just sit there with my hands folded and don't pay any attention," she explained.

"I think God knows that," I retorted.

Her face lit up, she threw her head back, and burst out laughing. When she had caught her breath she started laughing again. "Well, the priests know who I am," she continued. "They say, 'Hello Mabel.'"

"You know people in high places," I said.

Mom laughed harder. She must have laughed for ten minutes. The sound of her laughter lingered in the air like the clear notes of a cardinal's song. Both of us were changed by the laughter we shared that day.

A Cheerful Attitude

Many caregivers have little humor in their lives. But that doesn't mean caregivers should stop looking for it. Humor is an antidote for the dark times caregivers face.

Patricia Brown Coughlan discusses the importance of humor in her book, *Facing Alzheimer's*. Coughlan believes the act of maintaining a cheerful attitude helps caregivers to carry on in positive ways.

But Coughlan is careful to distinguish between a cheerful outlook and what she calls "brittle, false cheerfulness." We've all seen this falseness in action: you know, the smile that looks like it's held on with rubber bands.

I'm fortunate to have a mother who, despite the tragedies in her life, tries to retain a cheerful attitude. Mom's example serves me in good stead today, and I hope it will continue to do so through all of my tomorrows.

Reciprocal Body Language

The patient's body language is an information source for caregivers. In order to get out of the car, Mom swings her legs around (moving her right leg with her hand), puts her feet on the pavement, and does a little "dance" with her feet. Her dance tells me that standing up is a neurological challenge.

Similarly, the caregiver's body language sends messages to the patient. Many experts recommend touching patients on the hand. But caregivers should be cautious about touching patients who have fallen or have sores and bruises. Even a gentle touch may be too much.

Patients who are recuperating from surgery may fear being touched. After the metal socket was implanted, Mom kept saying, "Don't touch my shoulder." I needed and appreciated her reminders.

Some experts, including Deborah Tannen, believe women are called by their first names and touched more often than men. This kind of instant familiarity can be a sign of condescension. "Just as people feel free to touch, pat, and first-name children, they feel freer to use these friendly signs with women," she writes.

Asking permission is a safer and more considerate approach. For example, "May I give you a hug?" The patient usually agrees and hugs the caregiver back. Body language can get through to patients when other communication routes have failed.

Setting

Background Noise

Background noise must be eliminated or subdued if patients are going to hear our messages. Caregivers may not consider a churning washing machine or whirring dryer as background noise, but these noises are communication blockers. Television and radio noise also distract the patient's attention.

Over time, I realized the car radio distracted Mom from our destination and purpose. Perhaps her hearing aid distorts musical sounds. Anyway, I don't turn the car radio on anymore.

You may want to take an informal survey of the "noise pollution" in the patient's world: clanking dishes, scraping chairs, emergency beepers, moaning, vacuuming, dog barking, and so on. Identify the most distracting sounds and take steps to eliminate them.

Private Issues, Private Places

Private issues are best discussed in private places. A private setting helps keep things confidential and shows respect for the patient. But caregivers don't always have control over the setting.

When Mom was living in her studio apartment, we had a terrible confrontation in the lobby. I'd just told her a nurse would be delivering her daily medications to her. Mom seemed to accept the news and we left her apartment and got on the elevator. The head nurse walked by just as the elevator door opened.

"I don't need a nurse to give me my medicine," Mom shouted. "I'm not a child!"

"Yes, you need help, Mom," I responded.

"Why?"

"Because you don't remember to take your medicine," I replied. Mom looked bewildered. "Do you remember the x-ray that was taken of your brain? It showed the stroke damage."

"I don't care. I don't want a nurse," Mom said.

"Well, a nurse is going to help you," I concluded.

Despite her embarrassment, Mom pursued the topic and I pursued the solution. Each of us was determined to succeed. With the nurse's help, I managed to soothe Mom and get her to agree to the arrangement. However, everyone in the lobby witnessed the process.

Make the Patient Comfortable

Alzheimer's patients aren't very steady on their feet, and many use canes or walkers. The patient who is sitting in a comfortable chair will be more apt to receive our messages. Raising the patient's feet also may make him or her more comfortable. Some nursing homes have patients nap in reclining chairs rather than beds to help them distinguish between resting and going to sleep for the night.

Let the patient awaken fully before you discuss anything important. And make sure that the patient is warm enough and away from drafts. Most nursing homes keep the temperature at 72 degrees. If the patient complains about being cold, get him or her a sweater or a blanket. Then the patient can concentrate on language, instead of discomfort.

When Mom's feet get cold, she puts on a pair of my father's old golf socks. The socks are raggedy looking, but Mom treasures them. I think this connection with my father warms her soul as well as her feet. Mom misses Dad, and wearing his socks makes her feel closer to him.

Filling in the Blanks

Waiting for patients to fill in the blanks can make caregivers crazy. There are two opposing views on filling in the blanks. One view says doing so helps patients. The other view says it emphasizes the patient's waning language skills.

Because I'm a writer, I've filled in Mom's blanks without thinking, almost as if I was playing verbal scrabble. I realized Mom didn't appreciate this "service," so I've stopped filling in the blanks. Sometimes the silences are long, but that's the way it is.

Filling in the blanks for Alzheimer's patients may interrupt their thoughts and subject transitions. Each patient is different, so you will have to do what you think is best. In addition, caregivers need to learn the value of silence.

Values of Silence

Many caregivers are uncomfortable with silence. Research and experience have taught me to let silence "be." Gerald Goodman, Ph.D., and Glenn Esterly discuss "skillful silence" in *The Talk Book*. They say silence is a conversational skill with distinct benefits:

- Silence can open up tentative talkers.

- Silence can give the other person permission to speak.

- Silence can bring reluctant conversationalists back for more.

So the authors advise us to wait. The act of waiting serves several critical functions. Waiting gives the other person time to organize his or her thoughts. Moreover, waiting gives the other person time to come up with a "good answer."

Most of all, waiting is a sign of support, an indication that the listener is giving the speaker "deep attention." In short, the listener's mind isn't wandering but waiting for incoming messages.

I think of my mother's silence as punctuation—a comma, a dash, a dot, dot, dot. Sometimes her silence is a period. In my mind's eye I can see the period, a clear black dot against stark white paper. Leo Buscaglia, Ph.D., devotes an entire chapter to communication in his book, *Loving Each Other*. He asks listeners to be respectful of silences, and I think that's wise advice.

Reinforcement

The references I have consulted say caregivers should repeat their messages for emphasis. Think of repetition as verbal underlining or boldface.

While repeating messages helps some Alzheimer's patients, others pay no attention to it. Hearing specialists recommend rephrasing messages for patients who have a hearing loss. My mother responds better to rephrasing than to repeating. While I'm rephrasing a sentence, I usually shorten it as well. Succinct messages are more apt to be received.

Other kinds of reinforcement include phone calls, letters, reminder notes, videos, and the like. Written reminders will be more effective if you print the message (instead of writing) in large letters. Colored ink and stickers also help to get the patient's attention.

It's common for Alzheimer's patients to forget they've had visitors. A guest book will help the patient remember who has come to visit. However, the patient who has lost the ability to read won't get as much benefit from this.

Mom relies on an unusual written reminder—her charm bracelet. The jangling bracelet, which she wears day and night, has become part of Mom's personality. Each charm represents a grandchild and Mom checks the bracelet regularly throughout the day.

"I know my grandchildren's birthdays," she says confidently, "because they're all on the bracelet."

Social workers, activity directors, nurses, and nurses aides can also help to remind patients of events. In short, everyone benefits from a multimedia approach to reinforcement. The time will come, however, when nothing works.

Questions

Questions also show that you value the patient's company. In her book *The Dance of Anger*, Harriet Goldhor Lerner, Ph.D., calls questioning a "courageous act." I think asking a patient if he or she needs a new diaper takes a certain kind of courage.

An early childhood education technique has helped me to phrase the questions I ask my mother. Young children have difficulty choosing from too many options, such as one box of cereal from a four-shelf display. Alzheimer's patients are much the same. When I ask Mom a question, I limit her choices:

- "Do you want to wear the black blazer or the white one?"

- "Do you want to eat at our favorite restaurant or our house?

- "Would you like to give your friend a scarf or a pin?"

This may be the last chance family caregivers have to learn the answers to unanswered questions. The questions may involve genealogy or experiences or family secrets. Keep in mind, though, that some questions don't have immediate answers.

During a Christmas dinner, my mother started to eat a cork coaster. I rushed over to her. "What are you eating?" I asked.

"I don't know, but this homemade bread is tough as hell," Mom replied.

"You're eating a coaster," I explained. "Spit it out."

Immediately Mom stopped chewing and spit the dented, wet pieces of cork into my hand. The shock on her face quickly turned to bewilderment. "Why am I eating a coaster?" she asked.

This wasn't the time or place to answer her question. "I don't know," I replied.

The coaster is gone, but Mom's question lingers in my mind. More painfully, now I know the answer.

Coping With Anger

Being around angry patients is frightening for some caregivers. In *When Anger Hurts,* McKay and colleagues point out that observers cope with anger immediately and retrospectively. According to the authors, pushing another person's anger away psychologically—distancing—is one way of coping.

Distancing helps us to see the patient more clearly and to recognize that he or she is out of control. The authors say we also have the option of staying emotionally insulated and setting limits.

I set limits and made a list of conversational topics to avoid. At the top of my list are money, shopping, Mom's red coat, and her toaster. How did a toaster get to be such an explosive topic?

Well, it all started with the microwave. Mom put a can of pop in the microwave. The can exploded and caused a "meltdown" in the appliance, followed by a fire. Fortunately, Mom was able to push the microwave cart outside before the fire spread.

Naturally the director of nursing became concerned about Mom's safety. Her concern increased after Mom moved into her studio apartment. Not only did Mom leave the stove burners on, she left magazines, letters, and paper towels close to the burners. I was asked to disconnect Mom's stove and remove all electrical appliances.

After some negotiation, the director agreed to let Mom have her coffeepot. Later I replaced the drip pot with an electric kettle that shut off automatically. Mom adjusted to all of these changes, except the toaster, and that became her beacon of independence.

Nary a day went by without Mom asking for her toaster. She bought another toaster, which I also confiscated. "I'm going to report you!" she screamed.

I wasn't sure how to respond to this, so I agreed with her. "If it will make you feel better to report me, I suggest you do it," I said.

"I will," she said vehemently. "I need my toaster to fix waffles for breakfast. Do you think I don't know how to work a toaster?"

The fact is, she didn't know how to work a toaster. She would move the setting to high, and I would move it to low. To my knowledge, Mom never reported me, but she still talks about the toaster. And walking into our kitchen can set off the "toaster wars" again.

Written and Visual Information

As Alzheimer's disease progresses, caregivers and patients become dependent on visual reminders.

Mom was having trouble finding her apartment so I hung a wreath on the door. Other caregivers have decorated doors with flowers, a montage of family snapshots, or the patient's photo.

My brother and his wife send Mom a postcard from Florida each week. The postcards give her something to look at and a brief message to read. These cards, along with a magazine subscription, validate my mother. "I got mail today!" she exclaims.

Although nursing care subscribes to the newspaper, Mom wanted her own subscription. I consider the newspaper a prescription for optimism. My mother takes pride in having her own paper and cutting coupons from it. The newspaper connects her with the outside world.

Artwork

The twins generate an endless supply of artwork, now progressing from the scribble to the named scribble stage. "What's that?" Mom asked.

"Why that's a person, Mom," I said. "See, here's the body and here are two eyes."

"It's beautiful," she said with a chuckle. She studied the drawing intently. "You know it really is beautiful."

Artwork may be more than a decoration to Alzheimer's patients. The patient may rely on artwork, even wall colors, to mark the "trail" to his or her room. That doesn't mean they can find their way through a book, however.

Patients who have lost the ability to read may hold a book upside down. In *Facing Alzheimer's,* Coughlan writes that caregivers should ignore this fact and "not risk a bad reaction."

A lack of reading ability, however, doesn't mean the patient won't enjoy photographs. In fact, this may be the last chance family caregivers have to label family photos. As Leo Buscaglia, Ph.D., advises in his book, *Loving Each Other,* we don't have time to brood. Rather, we need to get on with living and loving.

Caregivers may wish to tape-record family stories. Filling in a family-tree book (available in bookstores) may also give the patient pleasure. The patient may find a measure of peace in dispensing family treasures. But these activities don't disguise the truth.

Finding the words is getting harder for patients and caregivers. Patients are in a process of decline, and caregivers are in a process of adjustment. Each is asking, "Do you hear what I hear?"

CHAPTER 8

Do You Hear What I Hear?

Topics

Divergent Speech

Memory Systems

Reality Monitoring

Boredom

Agitation

Emotional Self-Defense

Caregiver's Responses

How Scripts Help

Music Therapy

Alzheimer's as a Mental Illness

Dealing with Unresolved Grief

Where is Hope?

Wisdom of the Elderly

Divergent Speech

Patients and caregivers have different thoughts, and the result of these thoughts is divergent speech. The patient hears one thing and the caregiver another. Alzheimer's patients tell the most interesting, detailed, and inaccurate stories. They aren't lying but rather telling their version of the truth.

Suppose the patient tells a story about someone snatching food off his or her plate (which happens, by the way). Of course, the caregiver must investigate the story, and a story like this leads to all sorts of questions.

Is the story true? Is it partly true? Or is it false? Is the story a memory? Is it a blend of past and present? Is it a hallucination, a television plot, or an "adopted" story retold? The patient's story may be based on faulty memory and retrieval systems.

Other examples of divergent speech are:

Patient	*Caregiver*
"There's nothing to do."	"I plan a variety of activities."
"I'm lonely."	"The nursing home has a large staff and we visit often."
"I need to get out of here."	"I take Dad out several times a week."
"I can take care of myself."	"Dad needs more support services."

Patient	**Caregiver**
"I'm uncomfortable and cold."	"I'm giving her a nice bubble bath."
"I remember our trip out West."	"Wow, is he talking nonsense!"

Memory Systems

Humans have a variety of memory systems, according to David Mitchell, Ph.D., associate professor of psychology at Southern Methodist University in Dallas. Episodic memory is the recollection of events. Semantic memory includes vocabulary and general knowledge. Procedural memory (the most basic) is recollection based on stimuli, such as playing the piano or typing.

Reality Monitoring

Alzheimer's patients have trouble separating their thoughts from actual events, a process Dr. Mitchell calls "reality monitoring." In the severe and final stages of the disease, reality monitoring becomes more difficult.

"Did I take my medicine or just remind myself to take it?" "Did I eat lunch today?" "Was the check I wrote for this year's taxes or last year's?"

Reality monitoring taps memory storage and retrieval systems. With the help of Reed Hunt at the University of North Carolina and Frederick Schmitt at the University of Kentucky, Dr. Mitchell compared recall in young and older healthy adults with that of Alzheimer's patients. Study participants were asked to read certain sentences and complete others. A sample completion sentence: The gentleman opened the door.

Later the study participants were asked to differentiate between the two groups of sentences. The Alzheimer's patients could tell the difference only 50 percent of the time, the same as the chance flipping of a coin. This inability is a major difference between normal aging and Alzheimer's disease.

Giving the patient a short-term memory test is a way of measuring orientation. (See the Appendix for a sample test.) Before the test is given, the patient's hearing and vision should be checked. If the patient consistently fails to remember things like his or her address, phone number, and relatives' names, then orientation is poor.

According to Dr. Mitchell, some Alzheimer's patients have been helped by a process called "reality orientation." The foundation of this process is repetition. Around the clock, night and day, hour by hour, everyone who comes in contact with the patient repeats information. This is a challenging and tiring task for caregivers.

Verbal Wandering

Trying to follow disjointed conversations can make caregivers question their own reality. Roger Clem, of Lamar University, an expert on communication disorders attributes pointless conversations to "verbal wandering." The patient's inability to apply language rules confuses the listener even more.

Listening to verbal wandering is like listening to someone scan radio stations. You never hear an entire "song." The patient may verbalize his or her stream of consciousness in complete or partial sentences. A phrase, a word, a moan—there's no logic trail for the listener to follow. "Went there . . . my husband never did that . . . Oh, I'm so angry . . . Jennifer?"

To the listener, these conversations sound like nonsense, full of sound and fury and signifying nothing. What's more, verbal wandering disturbs other nursing home residents.

Although the caregiver doesn't understand the language the patient may expect a response. A general reply like "Thanks for telling me that" may help. We can offer the patient the comfort of listening, a vital and underused communication skill. We can also comfort the patient with a smile, a hug, a cozy blanket tucked around chilly feet.

Sometimes removing unnecessary stimulation from the patient's environment helps to cut down on verbal wandering. Caregivers have to balance overstimulation and understimulation, however. In time, we figure out the patient's tolerance level.

Lack of Introspection

Another process that requires the retrieval of memories is introspection. *Webster's Dictionary* defines introspection as the examination of one's own mental and emotional state. Introspection is a lost art for the patient who can't retrieve data. The patient is becoming less introspective, while the caregiver is becoming more so.

Mom and I used to discuss our innermost thoughts at the kitchen table. We sat in the cramped kitchen for hours, sipping coffee, munching coffee cake, and discussing the stuff of life. Surely, many of my values come from these times. I miss our introspective talks and the meeting of our minds.

Boredom

Patients who have lost the capacity for enjoyment are prone to boredom. Much of the boredom patients feel comes from memory loss. Bored patients get restless and wander from room to room.

In a sense, these patients are at odds with themselves. They want to do something but what can they do? Hobby skills such as knitting and woodworking may be gone, reduced to hazy memories. News broadcasts are a mishmash of information. Remembering names and words becomes increasingly difficult. The patient may be able to retrieve names after a struggle, a process some experts call "effortful memory."

No wonder patients sit and stare vacantly into space. Boredom must be twice as terrible if you can't remember the last time you were bored. My mother's boredom has caused arguments between us. She rarely participates in activities, spending her time watching television and reading the newspaper.

One day, after she saw a T-shirt ad in the newspaper, Mom became obsessed with shopping. She had staff members dial our phone number several times, and each call began with the sentence, "I need a black T-shirt."

"Why?" I asked.

"Well, I need a T-shirt to go with my black slacks," Mom said.

"You have lots of tops to wear with your slacks."

"Yes, but I don't have a black T-shirt," she insisted.

"You have so many clothes, they don't fit in your closet," I declared. "We're not buying you a black T-shirt." I knew Mom couldn't find a black T-shirt in her closet, and John and I had just bought her a new slacks outfit.

"Your medical expenses are increasing and this isn't a good time to buy a T-shirt," I said.

"That's my business!" she said loudly and that ended the phone call.

Boredom-Forgetting Cycle

The patient may participate in an activity and forget it a few minutes later. "All I do is sit," an elderly woman complained. "There's nothing to do here." But her nursing home has a top-notch activities program, and there's lots to do.

Choral groups come in and sing, and pianists give afternoon concerts. Regular exercise and story hours are scheduled. Less-impaired residents bake cookies together. Pets come and visit, and there are holiday celebrations and summertime picnics.

The patient hears the sentence, "There's nothing to do." But the caregiver hears the sentence, "I plan a variety of activities." Differences like these can lead to disappointments.

I thought I had planned a special day for Mom, a drive in the country and a visit with the twins, but things didn't work out as planned. The drive to our daughter's house takes a half hour. Mom fell asleep in the car and was groggy when we arrived. Five minutes later she asked to go home. After my daughter gave her a glass of iced tea, she reluctantly agreed to stay longer.

Mom sat on the deck in the bright morning sunshine and watched the twins play in the backyard. By the next week, the trip was forgotten and Mom was bored again. All of which proves the best plans can go awry. The boredom-forgetting cycle is ongoing.

Staff members and I are trying to get Mom involved in the activities program. She seems to want to be by herself, however, and her participation is minimal. Her nonparticipation may be a way of exercising control, a form of protest, a sign of fatigue, or a preparation for death.

Agitation

Alzheimer's patients often feel anxious and frustrated, and these feelings can build. The patient's ability to identify feelings decreases with time. Worse, the patient doesn't understand the cause of these feelings. Caregivers must be prepared for emotional outbursts and agitation.

Agitation is a physical response to feelings of frustration and includes these behaviors:

- prolonged pacing

- rattling doorknobs

- testing the bars on fire doors

- arm waving and pushing

- kicking

- grimacing and frowning

- darting eyes or dilated pupils

- loud speech and yelling

- "escape" language

The patient may say things like, "I've got to get out of here." A patient in the final stage of Alzheimer's may keep saying, "Out, out, out, out, out."

However, Frena Davidson, author of *The Alzheimer's Sourcebook for Caregivers*, says agitation may be a time of emotional clarity.

I know there are times when my mother has been agitated. Still, she has managed to come to terms with my father's alcoholism, the death of a child (my brother's twin), and her advanced age. Mom accepts life for what it is and believes she has lived at the best time.

Caregivers can communicate with agitated patients. Reassuring the patient is a good way to start, according to clinical psychologists Doreen Kotik-Harper and Robert Harper. Then turn off the radio or television (if they're on) and remove other patients from the area.

Above all, don't pressure the patient or make any demands. Use consistent verbal and nonverbal communication. This is one time when memory loss may work in the caregiver's favor, the psychologists note, and you may be able to redirect the patient.

Emotional Self-Defense

Failing patients use so-called defense mechanisms to protect their emotions. Defense mechanisms—and there are many of them—are behaviors that protect patients from the emotions of anxiety, shame, or guilt. I've seen patients use projection and rationalization, and they may use other behaviors as well.

Projection is the act of attributing your own traits, attitudes, and faults to others. For example, an angry patient may become convinced that the caregiver is angry also.

Rationalization is a way of justifying or explaining behavior. My mother forgot an afternoon party and explained the oversight by saying, "I didn't like the food they were serving so I didn't go."

Alzheimer's patients are in emotional pain, and we must let them express it. And this is precisely where many caregivers fail, says Davidson. We can listen to the patient's feelings and empathize with them.

"Shadowing"

"Shadowing," the practice of clinging or following caregivers, is also an emotional self-defense. The patient does these things because he or she feels insecure.

During a three-week stay at our house my mother followed me constantly. She stood behind me while I was preparing meals and followed me from room to room. I had an article due at the newspaper and was working in my office. Mom came downstairs and stood behind my chair, a bewildered expression on her face. "What are you doing?" she asked.

"I'm writing an article," I said, trying to keep my concentration.

Mom moved closer and rested her hands on the back of my chair. Hoping she would lose interest, I fixed my eyes on the computer screen and kept typing. Five minutes passed, ten minutes, fifteen minutes, and Mom didn't move.

"Could you back up a bit?" I asked. She folded her arms and changed her stance, but she didn't move an inch. She stood so close to me, I couldn't think. Finally, I asked her to go upstairs and read until I was finished.

"Shadowing" can test a caregiver's mettle. You may literally have to pry the patient's fingers from your arm to extricate yourself. Adding a conciliatory sentence such as "I'll see you later" puts a better slant on the situation. Offering the patient a hot or cold drink may also work.

Miscommunication

Just because we interact regularly with a patient does not mean we're always going to get along with him or her. Deborah Tannen, Ph.D., author of *That's Not What I Meant!* believes increased contact also increases the chances for miscommunication.

Alzheimer's disease causes some patients to turn against family caregivers. One patient told her daughter, "I like her (the professional caregiver) better than you." Another said, "You never call me," which wasn't true. Mom tells people, "My daughter put me in here."

Family caregivers may feel betrayed by such comments. We need to keep in mind that aggression, both physical and verbal, is another defense mechanism. The patient is living in a confusing world, and hostile comments are a way of surviving in that world.

Caregiver's Responses

In *Facing Alzheimer's*, Coughlan points out that successful caregiving depends upon special qualities. The caregiver has to develop a sense of what can and can't be controlled, learn to speak up, and "overcome the need to be sweet and friendly."

This doesn't mean the caregiver is insensitive. In fact, the opposite is true. The caregiver has to be ultrasensitive and observant in order to fine-tune language.

What works in the severe and final stages of the disease?

Role-reversal

I've found it helpful to put myself in my mother's place. Finding the words is easier when I do this, and I have new respect for my mother. She has managed to retain some control over life, her innate beauty, and her dignity.

Distraction

Other chapters have referred to the distraction technique. Above all, the caregiver wants to avoid contradicting the patient. On the way to a bath the patient doesn't want to take, for example, you might comment about an upcoming birthday party.

Clarity

Alzheimer's patients take our sentences literally. If you say, "I'll run down to the store and get some milk," the patient may expect you to start running. So be clear. Observing my mother has made me more careful about the words I choose.

"Friendly" Speech

All too often, caregivers ask questions like "Do you know who I am?" or "What did you do yesterday?" Each question is a test for the patient. In *The Alzheimer's Sourcebook for Caregivers,* Davidson says we should identify ourselves by name and refer to the last contact we had with the patient—church, store, dinner, or whatever.

Denial

Professional caregivers may deny the severity of the patient's disease. "I had a nice talk with your mother yesterday," a nurse told a family caregiver. The remark stunned the caregiver because her mother had been in a vegetative state for months. Nobody could have a conversation with this patient.

I asked a friend of mine, also a nurse, why a professional would say such a thing. She attributed the denial to three causes. First, professional caregivers may tell family members what they think they want to hear. In other words, the professional caregiver wants to spare their feelings.

Second, the caregiver might not be up to date on Alzheimer's disease. This is especially true of less-educated caregivers. In fairness, full work schedules, family responsibilities, and budget problems may prevent these caregivers from getting more education.

Third, denying the severity of the disease blocks out pain. The professionals, too, have to deal with grief while they're taking care of a terminal patient. Even when death is near, they keep trying. Denial may be an unconscious validation of their efforts.

Is a New Category Needed?

Family caregivers also practice denial and may become emotionally numb to avoid pain. Some adopt this attitude very early in the disease. A newly proposed category of dementia may help family and professional caregivers to combat this tendency.

Glen Smith, Ph.D., recommended a new dementia category at the Mayo Clinic's first conference on Alzheimer's. The category would be called "mild cognitive impairment." Dr. Smith diagrammed its placement this way:

Normal➔ Mild Cognitive Impairment➔Dementia

Only time will tell if this category will be established. Other experts have divided the severe stage of Alzheimer's into early and late subcategories. I believe these actions will increase public understanding of Alzheimer's and help all caregivers track its progression.

How Scripts Help

Most of us have received phone calls from telemarketers who are talking from a script. The script saves the telemarketer time and effort. And writing a script forces the speaker to clarify thoughts.

Scripts can help caregivers find the words to express themselves. The script doesn't have to be written out like the ones telemarketers use; just thinking it through may be all that's needed.

Before I told my mother she was transferring to nursing care, I planned a script. I practiced the script aloud at home. My message was softened with the happy memory of a pleasant trip Mom and I shared. The message: You need more medical backup than I can provide. Planning the script helped, and our conversation went better than I expected.

If you decide to jump-start language with scripts, keep them short and don't waste time on lead-in sentences. Get to the point quickly and repeat it for emphasis. End the script with a clear summary sentence such as, "I'll pick you up at five o'clock this afternoon."

Always use respectful language. The combination of respectful language and a short script stack the communications odds in everyone's favor. Follow-up the script with phone calls and notes.

Music Therapy

The mind uses different neurological pathways to store music and lyrics. Country music star Mel Tillis told a story on a television talk show that illustrates this point. Tillis described how his house caught fire.

He wanted to alert family members but, because of his stuttering problem, he couldn't get a word out. In desperation he started to sing, "Our house is on fire." His song alerted family members, and everyone managed to escape.

Music gets through to Alzheimer's patients when words can't. A family caregiver went to visit her father in the hospital. He was near death and seemingly unaware of what was going on around him. When the caregiver started to sing a hymn, however, her father's hand twitched in response.

A patient in the severe stage of Alzheimer's walked up to a nurse, and announced, "I want to sing." They sang a children's song together. The serenade roused other nursing home residents from sleep and one of them smiled.

Many nursing homes have music therapy programs: piano music to liven up lunchtime, soothing afternoon concerts, and patient sing-alongs. But Frena Davidson, author of *The Alzheimer's Sourcebook for Caregivers,* believes much of this music is "patronizing garbage."

Davidson would like patients to hear quality music—classical, ethnic, and new age. Although this is a good suggestion, some patients may only respond to the music stored in long-term memory, like "Old MacDonald had a Farm."

Patients might also enjoy listening to taped music with earphones. Make sure you adjust the volume before you give the earphones to the patient, however. And then check the volume again whenever you switch to another tape.

Alzheimer's as a Mental Illness

Perhaps nothing makes the tragedy of the disease clearer than its inclusion in the *Diagnostic and Statistical Manual of Mental Disorders (DSM-IV),* published by the American Psychiatric Association. The DSM-IV says the disease is slightly more common in women.

Diagnostic criteria for dementia of the Alzheimer's type include topics discussed earlier: impaired memory, aphasia, apraxia, agnosia, and functional disturbances such as with planning and sequencing. Subcategories are also listed: with delirium, with delusions, with a depressed mood, and uncomplicated (which means none of the above).

Alzheimer's eventually can lead to severe mental illness. The trauma of taking care of a mentally ill person can haunt a caregiver. Gerontology consultant Nancy Gnaedinger says recovering from this trauma may take years "or forever." Contact a geriatric specialist or psychiatrist for tips on communicating with a mentally ill patient.

Support Groups

You might also want to join a support group. Check the Yellow Pages of your phone book for leads. The Alzheimer's Association has a network of groups nationwide. Support groups have many advantages, among them, learning about the disease and sharing experiences.

Groups aren't for everyone, however. I had participated in many groups in the past, and I didn't want to join another. Instead, I set aside time for myself and spent this time reading or trying new recipes. Like my mother, sometimes I have to be alone with my thoughts.

In *Getting Through,* Ostuni and Santo Pietro express their belief that caregivers have to keep in touch with people in the outside world—"outsiders" they call them. "Outsiders" may be other caregivers, friends, neighbors, religious groups, or health professionals. Communicating with "outsiders" gives the caregiver time to rest, regroup, and rethink.

Some caregivers need professional help—family or individual therapy—but won't ask for it. Asking for help is a sign of failure in their minds. However, Ostuni and Santo Pietro say asking for help is one of the most unselfish things a caregiver can do.

Grief experts have been especially helpful for some caregivers.

Dealing with Unresolved Grief

Anticipatory grief can continue for years. This lack of closure takes a heavy toll on the caregiver. "Is this the last time I'll see my father?" Each day the caregiver says good-bye.

The caregiver's grief can cause communication to become stilted. At a time when the caregiver needs to reach out to the patient, he or she may withdraw. The patient hears the sentence, "My son isn't acting very friendly." In contrast, the caregiver hears the sentence, "I'm going to burst into tears any minute." Unresolved grief will shut down communication if we let it.

Patients, too, may experience grief. Betsy was in her 90s and becoming more forgetful by the week. One of her recurring stories was about seat belts. The story always ended with the sentence, "He wouldn't start the car unless my seat belt was fastened." She told the story over and over again.

Weeks later Betsy added a poignant sentence to her story. "Ohhhhh, I miss my husband." This wasn't a story about car safety, it was a story about grief and loneliness.

Death is one of our "necessary losses," according to author Judith Viorst. She might say the child in me is denying my mother's mortality. Viorst explains that a child will search for a mother who has left the family. Similarly, a grieving person will search for a loved one.

Although the search is unconscious, it is revealed in random, and often useless, activities. Viorst believes delaying and avoiding mourning causes the grief process to become "disordered." This can get family caregivers into emotional trouble.

Rather than avoiding grief, we can accept it as part of life. Mom has signed a living will, and we discuss its stipulations openly. Painful as they are, words like "no unnecessary measures" are necessary, and Mom keeps telling me it's time for her to "check out."

Where is Hope?

"Taking care of my mother is worse than having junky kids," a family caregiver said. "Junky kids stand a chance of getting better, but Alzheimer's patients don't." Many caregivers are facing multiple crises. Where is hope?

- *Hope may be found in research.* At the Mayo Clinic conference on the disease, Dr. Ronald Peterson, M.D., Ph.D., said more research was needed to determine what constitutes Alzheimer's. What are the early predictors? Are there biological markers doctors could watch for? What is the role of amyloid, a protein deposited in the brain? Could an Alzheimer's profile be developed? What drug treatments work best? We don't know what medical breakthroughs the future holds.

- *Hope may be found in friendship.* Robert Veniga, M.D., author of *A Gift of Hope*, describes how friendship can heal a broken spirit. Helpful friends are curious, honest, good listeners, and "would never walk out on us," he explains. Moreover, friends can be objective when caregivers can't.

  Spending time with friends always recharges me. My friends have sustained me throughout the caregiving process, and I'm grateful for their help. Strangers have shared their stories with me; I'm grateful for their help as well. I'm also grateful for the new friends I've made along the way.

- *Hope may be found in living the moment.* Questions can divert us from the moment and prevent us from enjoying it. Rabbi Harold Kushner, author of *When Bad Things Happen to Good People*, describes the human tendency to ask "Why?" "Why did my father get Alzheimer's disease?" "Why did he get it now?" But Rabbi Kushner says sometimes there are no reasons for the bad things that happen.

Instead of spending our energy on questions, Rabbi Kushner suggests we look for ways to give meaning to the bad things that happen to all of us. One of the reasons I wrote this book is to give added meaning to my mother's life and mine.

Wisdom of the Elderly

Alzheimer's disease doesn't necessarily erase all of the wisdom patients possess. One evening Emma approached a nurse and said, "Now let me get this straight. I go to bed and you keep watch. Is that it?"

"Yes," the nurse replied. "You can go to bed now and I'll keep watch."

"Good," Emma said. With surprising energy, she turned her walker around and headed for her room. Despite her dementia, Emma has retained a concern for personal safety and the ability to trust others. Emma usually has a cheerful expression on her face.

Some Alzheimer's patients rediscover the simple pleasures of life, such as good soup, warm blankets, and sunny weather. Mom has retained the familiar role of mother and finds comfort in it. "Don't walk around barefoot," she says. "You'll catch cold."

Let's listen for the wisdom of the elderly and learn from it. If nothing else, Alzheimer's teaches us to appreciate life—each day, each hour, each moment. The challenge of finding the words leads caregivers in new directions. We can grow in ways we never dreamed.

EPILOGUE

The Challenge

Now you have a better idea of how to communicate with Alzheimer's patients. You know about perception differences, how to get your message across, personal communication barriers, outside interference, causes of speech damage, reception and transmission errors, and how the disease alters speech.

The need for this information will increase as the number of patients increases. Caregivers and patients are both searching for words, and the process can be painful. During the course of writing this book, there were many times when I had to stop writing and have a good cry.

Few writers have had the chance to observe someone with probable Alzheimer's disease for so long. When I started the book I had no idea the chapters would follow my mother's life so closely. I am fortunate to be my mother's daughter and to have written parallel to her life.

I am also fortunate to have the kind of mind that tape-records dialogue. Many of the topics I've discussed come from conversations I had with Mom. The dialogue makes research findings real and helps readers recall key points. Writing this book was such a marvelous project that I didn't want it to end.

The more I learned about communicating with Alzheimer's patients the more intrigued I became. But I became sick at heart when I read about "granny dumping," the practice of abandoning the ill and elderly in public places. "Granny dumping" is a growing problem, according to the American Association of Retired Persons (AARP). Maybe if these beleaguered caregivers knew more about Alzheimer's disease and communicating with patients, "granny dumping" would subside.

Meanwhile, the number of Alzheimer's cases keeps going up. While diseases such as AIDS are making newspaper headlines, Alzheimer's is quietly, steadily, and relentlessly taking its toll. Doctors estimate some 14 million Americans will have the disease by the year 2040. And many of these people could live very long lives. Some experts predict many human beings will live to be 110 years old.

The way we treat Alzheimer's patients could determine the survival of civilization. Are we going to be a caring society? Can we make long-range plans? Will we follow through on these plans? Answering questions like these takes time and money. Still, there are steps we can take today to help the victims of tomorrow, including:

• Educating the public

• Financing research

• Identifying and training new workers

• Increasing support services, including support for caregivers

• Designing and building new housing

• Linking generations together

• Improving communication

The last step, improving communication, is the cheapest and most immediate for caregivers. Alzheimer's disease is the most common form of dementia, but the tips I've described may be applied to other dementias as well. What's more, the tips could help you to communicate at home, at work, and in your community.

One Sunday evening, as I was leaving nursing care, I met an elderly woman. She was sobbing. "Are you sad?" I asked.

"Yes," she answered, looking around the room. Although it was only 6:30, most of the patients were asleep, several with their mouths open. Two patients were in a vegetative state. "I want everyone to wake up and be like they used to be."

A similar thought had entered my mind and the comment startled me. I put my arms around the woman and hugged her. "I'm sorry," I said.

She hugged me back. "You're so nice," she said. "I'm going to stick with you, and we'll do things together." She paused to take a shuddering breath. "But I want everyone to wake up and be like they used to be."

"Well, we can't fix everything," I said quietly.

"I know," the woman agreed. "But we can try."

It isn't easy for caregivers to find the words they want. Some days we succeed; other days we fall short of our goal. The important thing is that we're trying to improve communication. And we keep on trying because we care.

Appendix

Topics

Communication Tips

Short-Term Memory Questionnaire

Glossary

Communication Tips

Voice

- Keep your voice calm.

- Use a low, even pitch.

- Speak clearly.

- Communicate with songs and music.

- Be respectful of silences.

Style

- Use simple words and avoid slang.

- Keep sentences short.

- Ask "yes" or "no" questions.

- Signal changes in subject, direction, and so forth.

- Repeat message for emphasis.

- Rephrase message if patient is hard of hearing.

Body Language

- Make eye contact.

- Use open gestures.

- Avoid the raised, slapping gesture.

- Approach the patient from the front or side, not from behind.

- Respect personal space.

Place

- Eliminate background noise.

- Find a private place to talk, if necessary.

- Make patient comfortable.

- Avoid discussing problems in public.

Short-Term Memory Questionnaire

1 What did you have for breakfast?

2. What year is it?

3. What day of the week is it?

4. What is today's date?

5. Can you tell me what you did last Sunday?

6. I'm going to say the names of three cities and ask you to repeat them in a few minutes: Chicago, New York, Boston.

7. What is your address?

8. What clothes did you wear yesterday?

9. What is your telephone number?

10. What did you do yesterday?

Note: Doctors have been asking similar short-term memory questions for about 100 years. The way these questions are asked influences the patient's response. Family caregivers might want to "weave" these questions into conversation. Humorous remarks also help to relieve the patient's tension.

Glossary

Adult day care—
activity program for Alzheimer's patients and other older adults with physical or mental impairments. May include meals.

Adult foster care—
home placement for patients who do not yet need nursing care but require supervision.

Agitation—
nervous behavior, often characterized by pacing or wandering.

Agnosia—
failure to recognize sensory stimuli.

Alzheimer's disease—
a progressive and degenerative disease that causes brain cells to die; the most common form of dementia.

Analgesic—
nonprescription or prescription pain reliever.

Anomia—
difficulty in recalling or recognizing names.

Aphasia—
inability to use or understand words in speech.

Apraxia—
loss of coordination necessary to perform common tasks involving complex movements.

Assisted living—
combination of housing and support services, including cleaning, laundry, transportation, selected meals, activity programs, and health care.

Auditory agnosia—
inability to recognize words and environmental sounds.

Behavioral disturbances—
personality changes that affect the mind, activities, diet, sleep, and bladder control.

Backward chaining—
a cue process that involves showing the patient the final destination, close landmarks, and the farthest landmark.

Body language—
nonverbal communication including hand gestures, facial expressions, and movement.

Catastrophic reaction—
patient's refusal to cooperate or take action, such as taking a bath.

Circadian rhythm—
the body's natural sleep-wake cycle.

CT scan—
computerized tomography; a series of cross-sectional X-rays that are converted by computer to create a three-dimensional image of a body structure, such as the brain.

Dementia—
deterioration of mental abilities caused by degenerative brain disorder.

Delusions—
false beliefs that persist contrary to evidence and reason.

Dysarthria—
articulation problems that cause slowed or slurred speech.

Effortful memory—
difficulty in accessing names for specific objects that are perceived.

Hallucinations—
false sensory perceptions; seeing, hearing, or feeling something that doesn't really exist.

Hypersexual agitation—
inappropriate and excessive sexual behavior.

Incontinence—
loss of bladder or bowel control.

Misidentification—
inability to recognize friends, relatives, or one's own reflection.

MRI—
magnetic resonance imaging; an imaging process that creates "pictures" of structures within a person's body.

Nervous tics or mannerisms—
involuntary and often repetitive facial and body movements.

Normal aging—
change process all humans experience, including gray hair, wrinkling skin, diminished muscle tone, and general weakening.

Overmedicating—
excessive use of prescription and nonprescription drugs, resulting in sleepiness or mental confusion.

Paraphasias—
word substitution errors; a partial aphasia.

Plateau periods—
a period in which progression of Alzheimer's disease is slowed or temporarily stopped but not regressed.

Pragmatics—

language rules applied to usage, including body language.

Probable Alzheimer's disease—

diagnosis made on the basis of physical and mental evaluations of a patient, often by ruling out other possible causes; at this time, diagnosis of Alzheimer's disease can only be verified through autopsy.

Psychosis—

mental disorder characterized by losing touch with reality.

Reaction time—

time required to respond to stimuli.

Reality monitoring—

separating internal thoughts from external perceptions and actions.

Reality orientation—

routinely repeated reminders of such things as time, place, and significant others to keep the patient stimulated and in touch with reality.

Reminiscence therapy/training—

use of memories (scrapbooks, photos, etc.) to foster thinking and speaking.

Respite care—
in-home care for patients; allows primary caregiver time to rest or get away.

Self-grief—
mourning health losses, such as loss of vision, hearing, walking, bladder control, etc.

Shadowing—
patient behaviors of clinging or following someone closely.

Speech apraxia—
involuntary, uncontrollable speech.

Sundowning—
late afternoon or night wandering and delirium.

Tactile agnosia—
inability to recognize objects by feel.

Time delay—
length of time it takes for the patient to speak or act.

Tinnitus—
ringing or hissing sounds in the ears.

Verbal wandering—
pointless, nonsense language caused by mental confusion; trailing off in midsentence without completing the thought before moving on to a new one.

Visual agnosia—
inability to recognize objects, pictures, or colors.

Word blindness—
inability to read or recognize common symbols such as stop signs.

Word retrieval deficit—
inability to name a prenamed object.

Bibliography

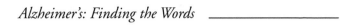

Aaronson, Arnold E., Ph.D.: Presentation to the Zumbro Valley Medical Society Alliance, Rochester, Minnesota, September 16, 1993.

Aaronson, Miriam K., Ed.D., Editor: *Understanding Alzheimer's Disease.* New York: Charles Scribner's Sons, 1988, pp. 130, 347.

Adams, Raymond D., M.D., and Victor, Maurice, M. D.: *Principles of Neurology, 4th edition.* New York: McGraw-Hill, Inc., 1989, pp. 381-389, 923-927.

Alpers, Bernard J.: *Clinical Neurology.* Philadelphia: F. A. Davis Company, Publishers, 1958, pp. 117-123.

Alzheimer's Association: Alzheimer's Disease (brochure). Chicago: Alzheimer's Disease and Related Disorders Association, Inc., 1987.

Alzheimer's Association: Alzheimer's Disease: Especially for Teenagers (brochure). Chicago: Alzheimer's Disease and Related Disorders Association, Inc., 1987.

Alzheimer's Association: Caregiving at Home (brochure). Chicago: Alzheimer's Disease and Related Disorders Association, Inc., 1987.

Alzheimer's Association: Is It Alzheimer's? (brochure). Chicago: Alzheimer's Disease and Related Disorders Association, Inc., 1987.

American Psychiatric Association: *Diagnostic and Statistical Manual of Mental Disorders (DSM-IV).* Washington, D.C., 1994, pp. 139-143.

Associated Press: From Diagnosis To Death, Alzheimer's Care Costs $213,000. *Physicians Financial News,* August 15, 1994, p. 40.

Associated Press: Reagan Reveals to Nation that He has Alzheimer's Disease. *Minneapolis Star Tribune,* November 6, 1994, pp. 1A, 2A.

Associated Press: Report: Elderly Suicides Traced to Complex Issues. *Rochester Post Bulletin,* August 15, 1994, p. 4C.

Baker, Beth: Outsmarting Alzheimer's: New Research May Speed Prevention Drug. *AARP Bulletin,* October 1994, pp. 1, 14-15, 17.

Barnhill, William: Self-Help Groups Bolster Alzheimer's Families. *AARP Bulletin,* March 1994, pp. 1, 15-17.

Bozzola, Fernando G., M.D. Gorelick, Philip, M.D., M.P.H. and Freels, Sally, Ph.D.: Personality Changes in Alzheimer's Disease. *Archives of Neurology,* March 1992, Vol. 49, pp. 297-300.

Burns, Alastair, Jacoby, Robin, and Levy, Raymond: Psychiatric Phenomena in Alzheimer's Disease. II: Disorders of Perception. *British Journal of Psychiatry,* July 1990, pp. 76-81, 1990.

Burns, Alastair, et al: Psychiatric Phenomena in Alzheimer's Disease. III: Disorders of Mood. *British Journal of Psychiatry,* July 1990, pp. 81-86.

Burns, Alastair, et al: Psychiatric Phenomena in Alzheimer's Disease. IV: Disorders of Behavior. *British Journal of Psychiatry,* July 1990, pp. 86-94.

Burns, David D., M.D. *Feeling Good.* New York: William Morrow and Company, Inc., 1980, pp. 184, 198.

Buscaglia, Leo F., Ph.D.: *Loving Each Other: The Challenge of Human Relationships*. New York: Fawcett Columbine, 1984, pp. 52-71, 65, 70, 154, 195.

Carroll, David L.: *When Your Loved One has Alzheimer's: A Caregiver's Guide*. New York: Harper & Row Publishers, 1989, pp. 16, 34-37, 119, 169-170.

Cavanaugh, Eunice, M.Ed., M.S.W.: *Understanding Shame*. Minneapolis: Johnson Institute, 1989, pp. 94-95, 130-131, 140-141.

Cohen, Donna, Ph.D., and Eisdorfer, Carl, Ph.D., M.D.: *The Loss of Self*. New York: W.W. Norton & Company, 1986, pp. 98-99, 152-154, 301.

Coughlan, Patricia Brown: *Facing Alzheimer's: Family Caregivers Speak*. New York: Ballantine Books, 1993, pp. 75, 79, 81, 146, 153, 211.

Curran, Dolores: *Stress and the Healthy Family*. San Francisco: Harper San Francisco, 1985, pp. 161-163.

Davidson, Frena Gray: *The Alzheimer's Sourcebook for Caregivers*. Los Angeles: Lowell House, 1993, 1994, pp. 37, 78-79, 98-99, 165.

Deutsch, Lynn H., et al: Psychosis and Physical Aggression in Probable Alzheimer's Disease. *American Journal of Psychiatry*, September 1991, pp. 1159-1163.

Dippel, Raye Lynne, Ph.D., and Hutton, J. Thomas, M.D., Ph.D., co-editors: *Caring for the Alzheimer's Patient*. Amherst, NY: Prometheus Books, 1991, pp. 77, 85-86, 88, 99, 100-109.

Drickamer, Margaret A., M.D., and Lachs, Mark S., M.D., M.P.H.: Should Patients With Alzheimer's Disease Be Told Their Diagnosis? *New England Journal of Medicine,* Vol. 326, April 1992, pp. 947-951.

Feldt, Karen, R.N.: Dealing with Alzheimer's: A Commonsense Approach to Communication. Film produced by Ramsey Medical Center, St. Paul, MN, 1990.

Friedman, Rita, Ph.D., R.N. and Tappen, Ruth N., Ed.D., R.N.: The Effect of Planned Walking on Communication in Alzheimer's Disease. *Journal of the American Geriatrics Society,* Vol. 39, July 1991, pp. 650-653.

Gallagher-Thompson, Dolores, Ph.D., et al: The Relations Among Caregiver Stress, "Sundowning" Symptoms, and Cognitive Decline in Alzheimer's Disease. *Journal of the American Geriatrics Society,* Vol. 40, August 1992, pp. 807-810.

Geewax, Marilyn: Idaho Case Highlights Tragic Problem of Alzheimer's and "Granny Dumping." *St. Paul Pioneer Press,* April 2, 1992, p. 11A.

Gnaedinger, Nancy: The Alzheimer's Household: Who Cares for the Caregivers? *Journal of the Canadian Medical Association,* Vol. 141, December 15, 1989, pp. 1273-1275.

Goodman, Gerald, Ph.D., and Esterly, Glenn: *The Talk Book: The Intimate Science of Communicating in Close Relationships.* Emmaus, PA: Rodale Press, 1988, pp. 28, 304-305.

Gruetzner, Howard, M.Ed.: Alzheimer's: *A Caregiver's Guide and Sourcebook.* New York: John Wiley & Sons, Inc., 1988, pp. 14-15, 39, 66, 86, 102, 108-109, 203-204, 215.

Golden, Daniel: Building a Better Brain. *Life,* July 1994, pp. 63-70.

Hiller, M.R.: Caring for Alzheimer's Patient Stressful. *Rochester Post-Bulletin,* Feb. 28, 1994, p. 20.

Horne, Jo: *Caregiving: Helping an Aging Loved One.* Chicago: American Association of Retired Persons (AARP) in conjunction with Scott, Foresman and Company, 1985, pp. 216-217, 249-250.

Hughs, John: Hope For Those With Alzheimer's Disease. *Rochester Post-Bulletin,* Oct. 22, 1993, p. 1A.

Hunt, Karen, Managing Editor: Tips for Talking With A Person With Alzheimer's. *Day by Day: Caring for Patients with Alzheimer's,* Fall 1993, p. 1.

Isselbacher, Kurt J., A.B., M.D., et al: Harrison's *Principles of Internal Medicine.* New York: McGraw-Hill, Inc., 1994, pp. 117-118, 138-141, 154-162.

Ivnik, Robert J., Ph.D.: Mayo Clinic consultant, phone interview on Sept. 21, 1994.

Jenike, Michael A., M.D.: Alzheimer's Disease.*Scientific American,* June 1991, pp. 1-5.

Jensen, Carl F., M.D.: Hypersexual Agitation in Alzheimer's Disease. *Journal of the American Geriatrics Society,* Vol. 37, Sept. 1989, p. 917.

Kim, Eun-Kyung: Woman Stranded Two Weeks in Van; Husband Missing. *Rochester Post-Bulletin,* Nov. 30, 1994, p. 4A.

Koss, Elizabeth, Ph.D., et al: Memory Evaluation in Alzheimer's Disease. *Archives of Neurology,* Vol. 50, Jan. 1993, pp.92-96.

Lerner, Harriet Goldhor, Ph.D.: *The Dance of Anger.* New York: Harper & Row, Publishers, 1985, pp. 190-191, 216-217.

Light, Leah L., and Burke, Deborah M., Editors: *Language, Memory, and Aging.* New York: Press Syndicate of the University of Cambridge, 1988, chapters 12 and 13.

Lukovits, Timothy G., M.A., and McDaniel, Keith D., M.D.: Behavioral Disturbance in Severe Alzheimer's Disease: A Comparison of Family Member and Nursing Staff Reporting. *Journal of the American Geriatrics Society,* Vol. 40, Sept. 1992, pp.891-895.

McKay, Matthew, Ph.D., Rogers, Peter D., Ph.D., and McKay, Judith, R.N.: *When Anger Hurts: Quieting the Storm Within.* Oakland, CA: New Harbinger Publications, 1989, pp. 44-45, 68-69, 150-151, 240-241.

Mace, Nancy L. and Rabins, Peter V., M.D.: *The 36-Hour Day.* New York: Warner Books, by special agreement with The Johns Hopkins University Press, 1989, pp. 45, 111-112, 118-120, 173-174, 180-181, 246.

Mason, Marilyn J.: *Making Our Lives Our Own.* San Francisco: Harper San Francisco, 1991, pp. 76, 176.

Mayo Foundation for Education and Research: 1st Annual Alzheimer's Disease Center Conference: For Family Members and Caregivers, Oct. 17, 1994.

Mayo Foundation for Medical Education and Research: *Clinical Examinations in Neurology.* Philadelphia: W. B. Saunders Co., 1957, pp. 231-243, 247.

Menninger, W. Walter, M.D.: Adaptation and Morale: Predictable Responses To Change. *Menninger Perspective,* Nov. 3, 1994, pp. 13, 15, 17.

Mortimer, James A., Ph.D. et al: Predictors of Cognitive and Functional Progression in Patients with Probable Alzheimer's Disease. *Neurology,* Sept. 1992, pp. 1689-1695.

Nalbantoglu, J., Ph.D. Lacoste-Royal, G., Ph.D., and Gauvereau, D., Ph.D.: Genetic Factors in Alzheimer's Disease. *Journal of the American Geriatrics Society ,* Vol. 38, pp. 564-567.

Nevid, Jeffrey S., Rathus, Spencer A., and Greene, Beverly: *Abnormal Psychology in a Changing World.* Englewood Cliffs, NJ: Prentice Hall, pp. 458-459, 460-467.

Ostuni, Elizabeth, and Santo Pietro, Mary Jo: *Getting Through: Communicating When Someone You Care for has Alzheimer's Disease.* Vero Beach, FL: The Speech Bin, 1991, pp. 12-17, 22-23, 28-29, 43.

Parke-Davis: *Caring for the Caregiver.* Morris Plains, NJ: Parke Davis, 1994, pp. 17, 79-80, 86.

Pinkney, Deborah Shelton: Before Their Time. *American Medical News,* March 14, 1994, pp. 11-14.

Pryor, Hubert: Theory Into Practice. *AARP Bulletin,* Oct. 1994, p. 12.

Ronch, Judah L.: *Alzheimer's Disease: A Practical Guide for Families and Other Caregivers.* New York: The Crossroad Publishing Company, 1989, pp. 72.

Rapesak, Steven Z., M.D., Kentros, Mary, M.D., and Reubens, Alan B., M.D.: Impaired Recognition of Meaningful Sounds in Alzheimer's Disease. *Archives of Neurology,* Vol. 46, Dec. 1989, pp. 1289-1300.

Raphael, Beverly: *The Anatomy of Bereavement.* New York: Basic Books, Inc., 1983, pp.50-53, 297.

Samuela, Martin A., M.D.: Something's Wrong with Dad: When Is It Dementia? *Emergency Medicine,* Nov. 15, 1990, pp. 65-97.

Shapiro, Pat: My House Is Your House. *AARP Bulletin,* Nov. 1994, p. 2.

Sunderland, Trey, M.D. , et al: Clock Drawing in Alzheimer's Disease: A Novel Measure of Dementia Severity. *Journal of the American Geriatrics Society,* Vol. 37, Aug. 1989, pp. 725-729.

Tannen, Deborah, Ph.D.: *That's Not What I Meant!* New York: Ballantine Books, 1986, pp. 39-40, 75-92, 96, 114, 180.

The Brain: Our Universe Within. Oct. 3, 1994, television special on The Discovery Channel.

Thill, Juliana: Learning to Live a Different Life. *Rochester Post-Bulletin,* Sept. 26, 1994, p. 1-C.

Veniga, Robert, M.D.: *A Gift of Hope.* Boston: Little, Brown and Company, 1985, pp. 154-179.

Viorst, Judith: *Necessary Losses.* New York: Ballantine Books, 1986, pp. 271, 280, 302.

Vitiello, Michael V., Ph.D., Bliwise, Donald L., Ph.D., and Prinz, Patricia N., Ph.D.: Sleep in Alzheimer's Disease and the Sundown Syndrome. *Neurology,* Vol. 42, July 1992, pp. 83-91.

Winstead, Mary: A Mother to Them All. *Minnesota Parent,* April 1992, p. 14-15.

Wolf-Klein, Gisele P., M.D., et al: Screening for Alzheimer's Disease by Clock Drawing. *Journal of the American Geriatrics Society,* Vol. 37, Aug. 1989, pp. 730-734.

Zubenko, George S., M.D., et al: Impact of Psychiatric Hospitalization on Behavior Complications of Alzheimer's Disease. *American Journal of Psychiatry,* Vol. 49, Nov. 1992, pp. 1484-1490.

About the Author

Harriet Hodgson has a B.S. degree in early childhood education, with honors, from Wheelock College, Boston, and an M.A. in art education from the University of Minnesota, Minneapolis. After a dozen years of teaching, Harriet decided to change careers and turned to writing.

An experienced nonfiction writer, Harriet is the author of 14 books for parents and children, plus many newspaper and magazine articles. She is also a contributing writer for the *Mayo Clinic Complete Book of Pregnancy & Baby's First Year.*

Harriet was both writer and narrator of "Parent Talk," broadcast on Minnesota Public Radio. A frequent radio and television guest, Harriet has appeared on more than 90 call-in radio programs, CBS Radio, WCCO Radio, many east coast television stations, and CNN. She is a freelance special features writer for the *Rochester Post-Bulletin.*

The mother of two grown daughters and grandmother of twins, Harriet lives in Rochester, Minnesota, with her husband John.

INDEX

CHRONIMED PUBLISHING
BOOKS OF RELATED INTEREST

Extraordinary Relationships by Roberta Gilbert, M.D. This revolutionary book, based on the innovative Bowen Family Systems theory, shows how to improve and fully develop our individual selves by improving our relationships, from friendships and family to the workplace.

004209   ISBN 1-56561-008-3 $12.95   ❑

Muscle Pain Relief in 90 Seconds by Dale Anderson, M.D. Now you're only 90 seconds away from relieving your muscle pain—drug free! From back pain and shin splints to headaches and tennis elbow, Dr. Anderson's innovative "Fold and Hold" technique can help. Simple, safe, and painless, this method is a must for all of us with muscle aches and twinges.

004257   ISBN 1-56561-058-X $10.95   ❑

Taking the Work Out of Working Out by Charles Roy Schroeder, Ph.D. This breakthrough guide shows how to easily convert what many consider to be a chore into enjoyable, creative, and sensual experiences that you'll look forward to. Includes methods for every form of exercise—including aerobics, weight lifting, jogging, dance, and more!
•A Doubleday Health Book Club Selection

004246   ISBN 1-56561-049-0 $9.95   ❑

Fight Fat & Win, Updated and Revised Edition by Elaine Moquette-Magee, R.D., M.P.H. This breakthrough book explains how to easily incorporate low-fat dietary guidelines into every modern eating experience, from fast food and common restaurants to quick meals at home, simply by making smarter choices.

004244   ISBN 1-56561-047-4 $9.95   ❑

Fight Fat and Win Cookbook by Elaine Moquette-Magee, M.P.H., R.D. Now you can give up fat and create great tasting foods without giving up your busy lifestyle. Born from the bestseller *Fight Fat & Win*, this practical cookbook shows you how to make more than 150 easy and tempting snacks, breakfasts, lunches, dinners, and desserts that your family will never know contain little or no fat.

004254   ISBN 1-56561-055-5 $12.95   ❑

Fast Food Facts, Revised and Expanded Edition by Marion Franz, R.D., M.S. This revised and up-to-date best-seller shows how to make smart nutrition choices at fast food restaurants—and tells what to avoid. Includes complete nutrition information of more than 1,500 menu offerings from the 37 largest fast food chains.

Standard-size edition, 004240   ISBN 1-56561-043-1 $7.95   ❑
Pocket edition, 004228   ISBN 1-56561-031-8 $4.95   ❑

Convenience Food Facts by Arlene Monk, R.D., C.D.E., with an introduction by Marion Franz, R.D., M.S. Includes complete nutrition information, tips, and exchange values on more than 1,500 popular name brand processed foods commonly found in grocery store freezers and shelves. Helps you plan easy-to-prepare, nutritious meals.

004081   ISBN 0-937721-77-8 $10.95   ❑

The Brand-Name Guide to Low-Fat and Fat-Free Foods by J. Michael Lapchick with Rosa Mo, R.D., Ed.D. For the first time in one easy-to-swallow guide is a compendium of just about every brand-name food available containing little or no fat—with complete nutrition information.

004242   ISBN 1-56561-045-8 $9.95   ❑

The Healthy Eater's Guide to Family & Chain Restaurants by Hope S. Warshaw, M.M.Sc., R.D. Here's the only guide that tells you how to eat healthier in over 100 of America's most popular family and chain restaurants. It offers complete and up-to-date nutrition information and suggests which items to choose and avoid.

004214   ISBN 1-56561-017-2 $9.95   ❑

Fat Is Not a Four-Letter Word by Charles Roy Schroeder, Ph.D. Through interesting scientific, nutritional, and historical evidence, this controversial and insightful guide shows why millions of "overweight" people are unnecessarily knocking themselves out to look like fashion models. It offers a realistic approach to healthful dieting and exercise.

004095   ISBN 1-56561-000-8 $14.95   ❑

Exchanges for All Occasions by Marion Franz, R.D., M.S. Exchanges and meal planning suggestions for just about any occasion, sample meal plans, special tips for people with diabetes, and more.

004201   ISBN 1-56561-005-9 $12.95   ❑

366 Low-Fat Brand-Name Recipes in Minutes by M.J. Smith, M.S., R.D./L.D. Here's more than a year's worth of the fastest family favorites using the country's most popular brand-name foods—from Minute Rice® to Ore Ida®—while reducing unwanted calories, fat, salt, and cholesterol.

004247   ISBN 1-56561-050-4 $12.95   ❑

All-American Low-Fat Meals in Minutes by M.J. Smith R.D., L.D., M.A. Filled with tantalizing recipes and valuable tips, this cookbook makes great-tasting, low-fat foods a snap for holidays, special occasions, or everyday. Most recipes take only minutes to prepare.

004079   ISBN 0-937721-73-5 $12.95 ❑

60 Days of Low-Fat, Low-Cost Meals in Minutes by M.J. Smith, R.D., L.D., M.A. Following the path of the best-seller *All-American Low-Fat Meals in Minutes*, here are more than 150 quick and sumptuous recipes complete with the latest exchange values and nutrition facts for lowering calories, fat, salt, and cholesterol. This book contains complete menus for 60 days and recipes that use only ingredients found in virtually any grocery store—most for a total cost of less than $10.

004205   ISBN 1-56561-010-5 $12.95 ❑

Beyond Alfalfa Sprouts & Cheese: The Healthy Meatless Cookbook by Judy Gilliard and Joy Kirkpatrick, R.D., includes creative and savory meatless dishes using ingredients found in just about every grocery store. It also contains helpful cooking tips, complete nutrition information, and the latest exchange values.

004218   ISBN 1-56561-020-2 $12.95 ❑

One Year of Healthy, Hearty, & Simple One-Dish Meals by Pam Spaude and Jan Owan-McMenamin, R.D., is a collection of 365 easy-to-make healthy and tasty family favorites and unique creations that are meals in themselves. Most of the dishes take under 30 minutes to prepare.

004217   ISBN 1-56561-019-9 $12.95 ❑

Foods to Stay Vibrant, Young & Healthy by Audrey C. Wright, M.S., R.D., Sandra K. Nissenberg, M.S., R.D., and Betsy Manis, R.D. From tips on increasing bone strength to losing weight, here's everything women in midlife need to know to keep young and healthy through food. With authoritative advice from three of the country's leading registered dietitians, women over 40 can eat their way to good health and feel better than ever!

004256   ISBN 1-56561-057-1 $11.95 ❑

200 Kid-Tested Ways to Lower the Fat in Your Child's Favorite Foods by Elaine Moquette-Magee, M.P.H., R.D. For the first time ever, here's a much needed and asked for guide that gives easy, step-by-step instructions to cutting the fat in the most popular brand-name and homemade foods kids eat every day—without them even noticing.

004231   ISBN 1-56561-034-2 $12.95 ❑

Chronimed Publishing

P.O. Box 59032
Minneapolis, Minnesota 55459-9686

Place a check mark next to the book(s) you would like sent. Enclosed is
$ _____. (Please add $3.00 to this order to cover postage and
handling. Minnesota residents add 6.5% sales tax.)

Send check or money order, no cash or C.O.D.'s. Prices and availability are
subject to change without notice.

Name_____

Address_____

City _____State _____Zip_____

Allow 4 to 6 weeks for delivery.
Quantity discounts available upon request.

Or order by phone: 1-800-848-2793,
612-546-1146 (Minneapolis/St. Paul metro area).
Please have your credit card number ready.